# TWENTIETH CENTURY QUILTS
# 1900-1950

"Paradise Garden." Made by Rose G. Kretsinger. 1945. Emporia, Kansas. 94½" x 93". The superb appliqué and stuffed work accomplished by Mrs. Kretzinger and her helpers rival the finest work of quilters a century ago, when pride in one's needlework was a woman's joy. An astonishing array of color and decorative detail emanate from the center of this floral kaleidoscope. The design was inspired by a quilt made in Maryland in 1857 by Arsinoe Kelsey Bowen, and recalls the earlier majestic appliqués attributed to Maryland quiltmaker Achsah Goodwin Wilkins (1775–1854). (Spencer Museum of Art, The University of Kansas; Gift of Mary Kretsinger)

# TWENTIETH CENTURY QUILTS 1900-1950

## Thos. K. Woodard & Blanche Greenstein

E.P. Dutton   New York

To the twentieth-century quilters
whose legacy will remain
a source of pleasure and inspiration
for centuries to come

INTERVIEW WITH FANNIE B. SHAW

We spoke with Mrs. Shaw, who at the present writing is over 90 years old and lives in Van Alstyne, Texas. She recalled very clearly how she came to make this extraordinary quilt.

"My inspiration came from Herbert Hoover. Every time you picked up the paper or heard the radio he would talk about good times around the corner. He would make it sound so good. I wondered could I make a picture of what he was saying and what he meant. I went to bed one night and couldn't get it off my mind. I thought a quilt would show all people from all walks of life. Many years later my granddaughter took the quilt to show and it won first prize.

"The quilt had educated me again.... I can't put a price on the quilt. It is history to me and I made it myself. Every block I made is different. The two most interesting are the cowboy and the bum. The bum with patches on his clothes came by asking for a handout during the Depression. He came up to our porch. My husband and I were farmers. My husband had a real bad cold and had to go out and get some wood. It was drizzling and freezing. The man came up to the porch and knocked on the door. My husband said, 'I'm sick, and if you'll go and chop up wood, I'll give you a meal.' The man just turned and walked off. That's where I got my idea about the bum peeping around the corner. How he was dressed.

"Cowboys had to sell their horses to help their families out. Chaps on and a bandana handkerchief....

"Every block had 35 to 40 pieces. There are 900 to 1000 pieces in the quilt. Two women wrote for a pattern. There is nobody that would make this quilt but me. It took over two years to cut the pattern and make the quilt: 1930–1932."

NOTE: Mountain Mist, formerly associated with Stearns & Foster, is now a brand name in the Consumer Products Division of the Stearns Technical Textiles Company.

Copyright © 1988 by Thos. K. Woodard and Blanche Greenstein. / All rights reserved. / No part of this publication may be reproduced or transmitted in any form or by any means, electronic or mechanical, including photocopy, recording, or any information storage and retrieval system now known or to be invented, without permission in writing from the publisher, except by a reviewer who wishes to quote brief passages in connection with a review written for inclusion in a magazine, newspaper, or broadcast. / Published in the United States by E. P. Dutton, a division of NAL Penguin Inc., 2 Park Avenue, New York, N.Y. 10016. / Published simultaneously in Canada by Fitzhenry & Whiteside, Limited, Toronto. / W / Library of Congress Catalog Card Number: 86-71622 / Printed and bound in Spain. / ISBN: 0-525-24244-9 (cloth); ISBN: 0-525-48115-X (DP).
10 9 8 7 6 5 4 3 2 1   First edition

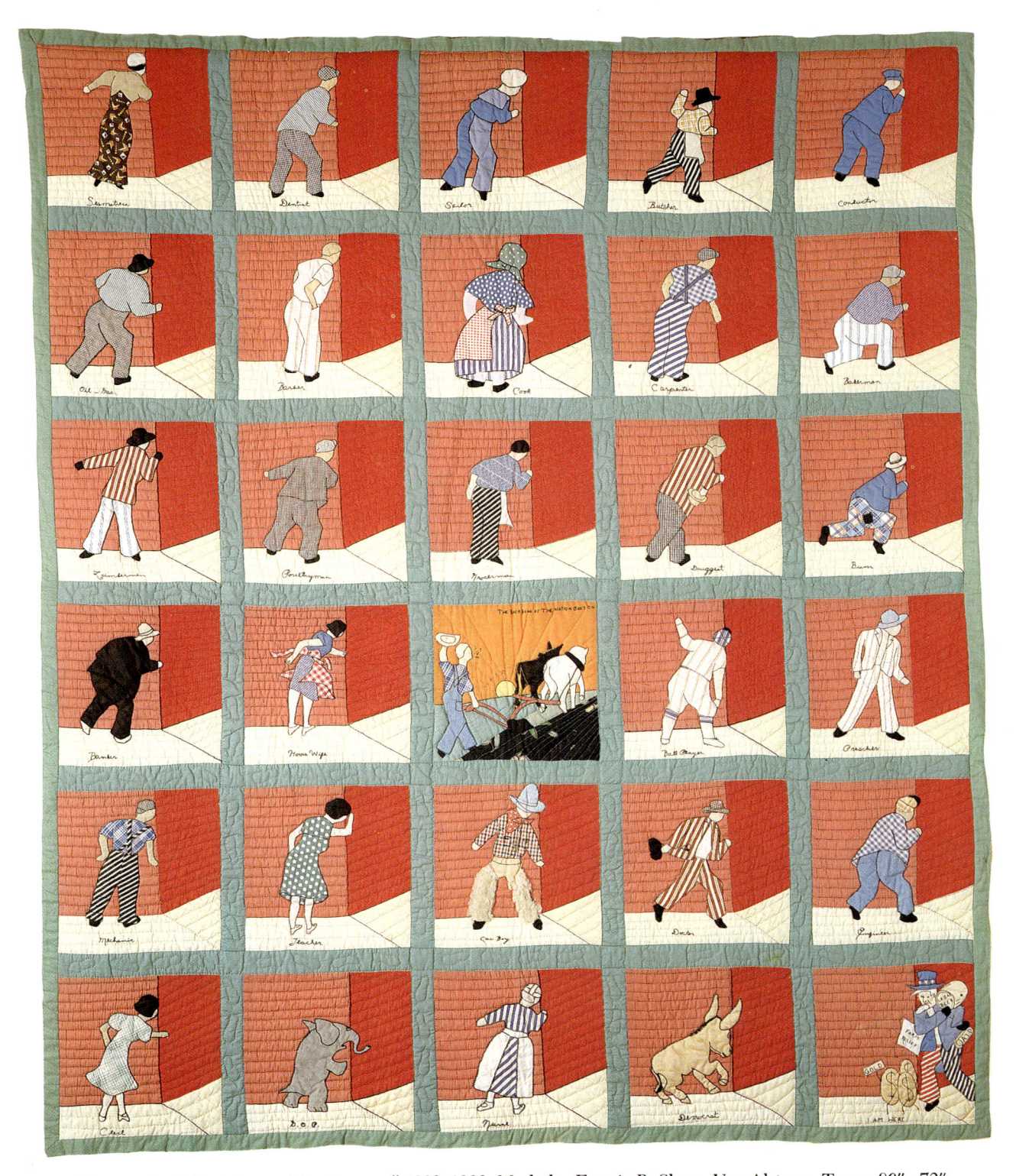

"Prosperity Is Just Around the Corner." 1930–1932. Made by Fannie B. Shaw, Van Alstyne, Texas. 86" x 72". Among the characters looking around the corner for President Hoover's promise are the preacher, the barber, the bum, and the housewife, whom quilter Fannie Shaw thought of as herself. At the bottom right corner, Uncle Sam arrives bearing "farm relief," "legal beer," and "aid," just as Hoover predicted. Photograph courtesy Nancy Hawkins.

# ACKNOWLEDGMENTS

Our very special thanks go to:

Claire Whitcomb, writer, whose formidable contributions to this project included organizing our research, clarifying and articulating our early manuscripts, invaluable assistance with composition, and, most of all, helping us get to the point;

Cuesta Benberry, quilt historian, for making available her vast storehouse of material on twentieth-century quilts that she has collected for many years with unbridled enthusiasm, as well as her own expertly written essays and articles on the subject;

Barbara Brackman, quilt historian, whose comprehensive *Encyclopedia of Pieced Quilt Patterns* served as an invaluable source for pattern identification;

Bonnie Leman, founder and editor-in-chief of *Quilter's Newsletter Magazine*, the monthly publication that has brought quilting news and patterns to quilters throughout America for over a quarter of a century;

Joyce Gross, editor of *Quilter's Journal*, a scholarly periodical about people and events that have contributed to the world of quilting in America;

Schecter Lee, photographer;

and, Cyril I. Nelson, our editor, to whom we are deeply indebted for his assistance and encouragement in the completion of this book.

And to the following who generously provided their quilts for photography, or who supplied color transparencies, information, and treasured reminiscences about twentieth-century quilting: Taya Allison; Dana Alpern; Enid Alpern; Annette and George Amann; America Hurrah Antiques, New York City; Oscar Appel; The Art Institute of Chicago, Chicago, Illinois; Joyce Aufderheide; Joyce Bacon; Judy Lawry Ball; Mr. and Mrs. Howard T. Barnett; Marilyn and Arnold Baseman; Edwin Binney III and Gail Binney-Winslow; Robert Bishop; Harriet and Bruce Blank; Jon Blumb; Maura and Lee Blumenthal; Doni Boyd; Jane Braddock; Marilyn and Milton Brechner; Karey Bresenhan; Diane and Clyde Brownstone; Ken Burris; Captain Tryon Antiques; Helen and Robert Cargo; Kate Christopherson; Patricia Coblentz; Judy Corman; Susan and David Cunningham; Muffin Cunnion; Mrs. Artie Fultz Davis; Imelda DeGraw; The Denver Art Museum, Denver, Colorado; Sanna Deutsch; Janet Dreiling; Nancy Druckman, Sotheby's, New York City; Chris Edmunds; Nora Ephron; Kathy and Fred Epstein; Rochelle Epstein; Helen Ericson; Esprit Collection, San Francisco, California; Pat Ethridge; Pat Ferrero; Christi Finch; M. Finkel & Daughter, Philadelphia, Pennsylvania; Laura Fisher, New York City; Marie and Thomas Foster; Kathy and Frank Gaglio; Galerie St. Etienne, New York City; Heather and Charles Garbaccio; Sally Garoutte; Betsey and Wendell Garrett; Pat and Rich Garthoeffner; Mariette Gomez; Elizabeth Hagerman; Roy Hale; Donna and Bryce Hamilton; Nancy Hawkins; Gail and Jonathan Holstein; Honolulu Academy of Arts, Honolulu, Hawaii; William N. Hopkins; Carter Houck; Gay Imbach; Elizabeth Ingber; Barbara Johnson; Kelter-Malcé Antiques, New York City; Elizabeth and Richard Kramer; Beverly Labe; Mr. and Mrs. Ronald Lauder; Noreen Lewandowski; The Library of Congress, Washington, D.C.; Sarah E. MacNeil; Heather MacCrae; Jo and Frank McClure; Kim McKim; Marsha and Jay Mendel; Sue Ellen Meyer; Judith and James Milne, New York City; Minnesota Historical Society, St. Paul, Minnesota; Bettie Mintz; Polly Mitchell; Sandra Mitchell; Kathy Molnar; Museum of American Folk Art, New York City; Helen Pearce O'Bryant; Betty Osband; Susan Parrish, New York City; Mr. and Mrs. Jerome Pustilnik; Pamela Reising; The Franklin D. Roosevelt Library, Hyde Park, New York; Joanna S. Rose; Stella Rubin; Stella Saltonstall; Joe Sarah; Mary Schafer; David Schorsch; Laurie Schwarm; Sears, Roebuck and Co.; Fannie B. Shaw; Robert Shaw; Shelburne Museum, Shelburne, Vermont; Marie Shirer; Viola Shirer; Cathy Shoe; Carol Shope; Julie Silber; Merry Silber; Gerry Lou Silverman; Laurene Sinema; Madeline Smith; Smithsonian Institution, Washington, D.C.; Ruth Snyder; Sotheby's, New York City; Spencer Museum of Art, The University of Kansas, Lawrence, Kansas; Star of the Republic Musuem, Washington, Texas; Nancy and Sam Starr; Stearns & Foster, Cincinnati, Ohio; Mr. and Mrs. Robert Steinberg; Olga Stephen; Betty Sterling; Eve Stuart; Sweet Nellie, New York City; Beverly Swihart; Lenore Swoiskin; Pearl Thate; Billie Thornburg; Sandra Todaro; Joan Townsend; Louise O. Townsend, *Quilter's Newsletter Magazine*; Frances Stenge Traynor; Marilyn Trent; Anita Trotta; Helaine Van Oosten; Wild Goose Chase Quilt Gallery, Evanston, Illinois; Lanford Wilson; Marna Wilson; Jo A. Wood; Frances Woodard; Nellie Snyder Yost.

# CONTENTS

| | |
|---|---|
| Foreword | ix |
| Introduction | 1 |
|     The Great Quilt Revival | 7 |
|     A Folk Art Grows Up | 10 |
|     Design Sources | 12 |
|     Worldly Things | 17 |
|     Patterns for Sale | 18 |
|     Paint by Number | 21 |
|     And the Winner Is… | 23 |
|     The Pros | 25 |
|     And in This Corner… | 26 |
|     Kitsch as Kitsch Can | 29 |
|     Not for Women Only | 32 |
|     Flights of Fancy | 33 |
|     Changing Times | 34 |
|     Collecting Twentieth Century Quilts | 36 |
|     Displaying Twentieth Century Quilts | 37 |
|     Quilt Care | 38 |
| Notes | 39 |
| A Gallery of Twentieth Century Quilts | 41 |
|     Flowers that Bloom in the Spring | 43 |
|     Objects of My Affection | 63 |
|     Round and Round | 68 |
|     Shining Stars | 74 |
|     A Tisket, a Tasket | 79 |

| | |
|---|---|
| Home Sweet Home | 83 |
| People and Progress | 88 |
| Graphically Speaking | 93 |
| My Country, Tis of Thee | 98 |
| Going to Pieces | 106 |
| One Picture Is Worth 1,000 Words | 113 |
| Changing the Subject | 122 |
| For Children of All Ages | 128 |
| Flights of Fancy | 133 |
| Bibliography | 139 |
| References | 141 |
| Index | 147 |
| About the Authors | 150 |

# FOREWORD

In writing the first comprehensive book on the history of twentieth-century quilts, Thos. K. Woodard and Blanche Greenstein reveal that there exists a fundamental lack of knowledge about the *continuing* tradition of quiltmaking. Twentieth-century quilts are the least-documented quilts in American history. So there was a compelling need for *Twentieth Century Quilts: 1900–1950* to be written.

As the authors began their research, they met with some challenges, occasionally surprising ones. They encountered a voluminous amount of material—a surfeit of riches. The investigator's usual complaint is that there is a dearth of available information, so it may be difficult to appreciate the concern of a researcher who has found too much. However, the majority of this raw data was uncatalogued, and so an extensive culling, organizational, and selection process was necessary. How to establish limits and still present a nonskewed version of quiltmaking in this heretofore undocumented fifty-year span was indeed a formidable task. Also, the history about which Woodard and Greenstein were writing was so recent, they frequently had doubts about whether or not they could maintain the proper perspective on this period. Woodard and Greenstein met each of those challenges with perseverance, courage, and vigor.

Today, there is abundant historical information about the splendid quilts of the eighteenth and nineteenth centuries. Whereas the authors stress the continuation of the quiltmaking tradition into the twentieth century, they do not suggest that the modern quilt is a weakened or inferior descendant. In fact, the authors do not indulge in invidious comparisons. Instead, they place the twentieth-century quilt in its own historical context. Woodard and Greenstein carefully link the changes in the way early twentieth-century quilts were made, how they look, and the reasons for making them to the artistic, social, and political environments of the years 1900 to 1950.

A central theme in this book is the importance of the published quilt pattern in the twentieth century, and its almost universal use. The authors differentiate between a quilt kit and a published quilt pattern, a difference that is often blurred in the minds of some people. The use of the published quilt pattern did profoundly affect quiltmaking in America. Its use brought a system of checks and balances—disadvantages counterbalanced by advantages—a topic fully explored by the authors. Then cutting through all of the pros and cons of published pattern use, Woodard and Greenstein uncovered in masterly fashion the single effect that has had the most far-reaching consequences nationwide for twentieth-century American quiltmaking.

*Twentieth Century Quilts: 1900–1950* is prime evidence that a quilt text founded on historical accuracy and attention to detail need not be dull and tedious. This book discloses that the story of twentieth-century quilts is different, yet fascinating, and often amusing. There are readers who can remember some of the events cited in this book, and who will smile at the remembrance. There is a promise here to the readers that they will be enlightened, enriched, and entertained by this monograph. Woodard and Greenstein's research and book serve as a beacon to light the way to a period shrouded by both a lack of appreciation and an understanding of its quiltmaking activities. Welcome to the light!

CUESTA BENBERRY

"Center Medallion." Inscribed: "A Y 1937." New Jersey. 96" x 88". Strong evidence that the love of fine quilting never left the consciousness of women skilled at needlework is easily found in this twentieth-century masterpiece. The hallmarks of magnificent quilts of the nineteenth century are all present in this piece: from the delicate appliqué and elaborate quilt stitchery—including trapunto or stuffed work—to the compelling use of color, exotic subject matter, and skillfully balanced composition.

# INTRODUCTION

The first five decades of the twentieth century witnessed a fascinating and relatively unexplored flourish of quiltmaking, and they are framed by two strong images. One is of the Victorian lady who, on New Year's Eve 1899, lifted her glass to the new century. She wore a dress that brushed the floor, rode in a horse-drawn carriage, dined by gaslight, and knew all too well why laundry day was called "blue Monday." The other image is of the modern woman who toasted the year 1950. She drove a car, watched television, illuminated her house with the flick of a switch, and bought almost everything she owned in a store. These two images are parentheses around a period of great change, when women gained the important right to vote and also acquired all types of leisure-creating home appliances. Some of the domestic arts of their grandmothers were left behind, but one traditional and favorite pastime of American women—quilting—remained an important household activity. For two full decades—the 1920s and 1930s—the twentieth century saw the revitalized art of quilting grow to the proportions of a national passion.

To gauge the intensity of interest in the making of patchwork, it is useful to compare those years to the present. Since the Bicentennial, we have been experiencing another period of enthusiasm for quilts, fueled in part by the immense popularity of American "country-style" decorating. Recently, for example, the annual blockbuster Houston Quilt Festival in Texas attracted a formidable 20,000 quilt aficionados from every state and twenty foreign countries. In 1933, however, a Mountain Mist quilt exhibit in Detroit opened its doors to 50,000 people in three days.[1] Also in 1933, Sears, Roebuck put a two-by-three-inch notice in its January catalogue, heralding a quilt competition in honor of Chicago's Century of Progress fair. By May 15, they had nearly 25,000 entries vying for a $1,000 prize, plus $200 if the quilt reflected the Century of Progress theme. The crowning attraction: the winning quilt would be given to First Lady Eleanor Roosevelt.[2] In 1977, *Good Housekeeping* announced a quilt contest with a $2,000 prize and over 9,000 entries poured into its offices.

From the beginning of the century, the quilt bandwagon had a number of diverse riders. Periodicals such as *The Ladies' Home Journal* offered patterns that proved immensely popular with its readership. By the twenties, some magazines began selling or giving away quilt kits as subscription incentives. Newspapers, including the *Kansas City Star*, responded to reader demand in the late 1920s and began running regular columns featuring patterns. By the early 1930s, a Gallup survey of six major city newspapers found the Sunday quilt articles to be the papers' single most-popular feature, attracting thirty-two percent of women readers.[3] Finally, department stores discovered that quilting was a lucrative means of selling fabric and other dry goods. Even Macy's, the most powerful of the department stores, supported quilting. In 1932, it booked Mrs. Scioto Danner of Kansas to show her quilts and patterns for two weeks, even though, according to Mrs. Danner's memoirs, many New York

1. *Portrait of My Mother Making a Quilt.* Nan Phelps. 1947. Oil on canvas. 59⅝" x 44½". Sitting by a table covered with a crewel-embroidered cloth, Nan Phelps's mother pieces a "Dresden Plate" quilt, one of the three most popular patterns of the twentieth century. In her work basket, additional patches are at the ready. (Copyright © 1981, Galerie St. Etienne, New York)

2. Photograph of a quilter. November 1914. An oil lamp, pet goldfish, a family bible, a calendar hanging on the wall, and a "Roman Stripes-Log Cabin" variation in progress tell us much about the life of this anonymous quilter. (Marilyn and Arnold Baseman)

3. A treasure trove of contest entries is examined with a magnifying glass by Sears, Roebuck's E.J. Condon (left) and George Vidal, whose employer had $7,500 to distribute among winners of their Depression-era contest in 1933. 24,878 quilts were sent to Sears by hopeful quilters across the nation. Photograph courtesy Sears, Roebuck and Co.

4. *Needlecraft Magazine*. September 1928. The art and romance of quilting helped sell magazines, such as *Needlecraft*, at ten cents an issue. This copy was mailed to a subscriber in Illinois. Photograph courtesy Cuesta Benberry.

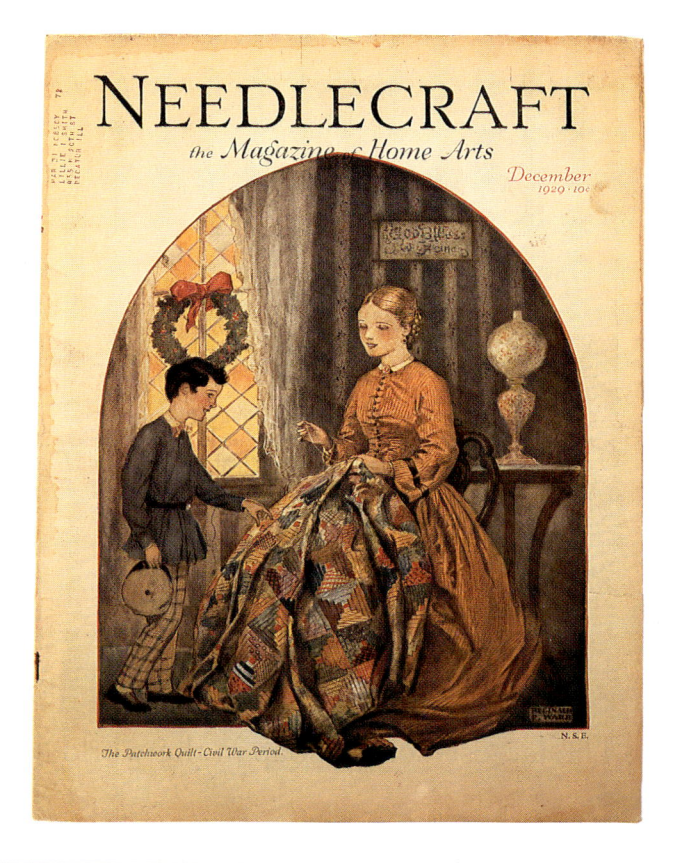

5. *Needlecraft, the Magazine of Home Arts*. December 1929. In 1929, the old-fashioned art of quilting was generally taught in a very modern way—through magazines such as *Needlecraft*. Editors, however, captured the nostalgic appeal of quilting by evoking grandmother's era, as in this Civil War scene where a young son points proudly to his mother's fine handiwork, a "Log Cabin-Courthouse Steps" variation worked in wool challis. Photograph courtesy Cuesta Benberry.

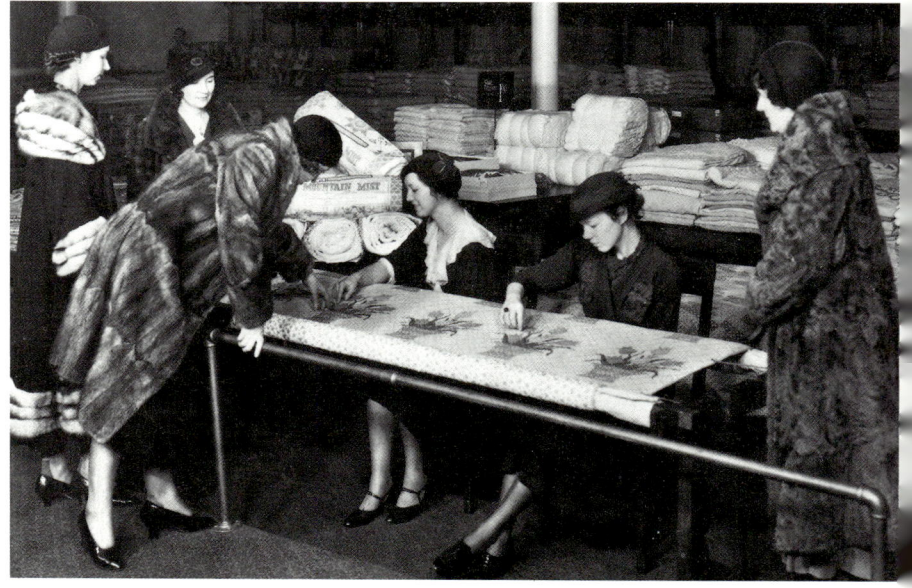

6. Stearns & Foster quilting demonstration. Ca. 1932. To boost sales of its Mountain Mist batting, Stearns & Foster held department-store quilting demonstrations that attracted even fashionable women of the 1930s. Photograph courtesy Stearns & Foster.

women didn't know what a quilt was and asked if it were some sort of a table pad. Mrs. Danner's display was a success nonetheless. Customers drawn by a street-window display and a Sunday ad lined up for an hour to make purchases. After that, Mrs. Danner was wooed by every major department store in the country and was booked two years in advance, employing six crews of two girls each to meet the demand.[4]

Besides being good business, quilting was also good government policy. In the Depression, the WPA (Works Progress Administration) sponsored programs to encourage arts and crafts, including quiltmaking. One of the states that had a WPA Statewide Museum Extension Project was Pennsylvania, where Ruth Finley, author of a 1929 book on quilting, acted as adviser for quilt patterns and quilting techniques in South Langhorne and Croydon. WPA, employing out-of-work artists, produced portfolios of quilt patterns painted in their actual size that were intended to be part of the Index of American Design.

The WPA Index of American Design (1935–1940) was the most massive government-sponsored project ever attempted to record such early American decorative arts as Shaker furniture, folk-art paintings, toys, and textiles, including quilts. Of the thirty-five states that participated, the majority had a quilt-rendering group.

In the New York City Project of the Index, at least 100 paintings or renderings of quilts, quilt squares, and quilt details were produced. The Southern California Project at Los Angeles produced even more. Records of the quilt's maker, materials in the quilt, date, provenance, the quilt's owner/lender, and occasionally the pattern name were kept. Today those records, although they were not uniformly kept at all project locations, may represent the only documentation available about some of the quilts.

In the period 1940 to 1960, authors of quilt books and quilt articles in periodicals used the Index renderings of quilts as illustrations, rather than photographs of the actual quilts.

Some of the people affiliated with the Index as artists, project directors, cooperative lenders, or supporters are names we recognize as being important in twentieth-century quilt history, such as Suzanne Chapman of the Museum of Fine Arts in Boston, Frances Lichten of Pennsylvania, Mrs. Danner, Suzanne Roy, and Florence Peto.

Unfortunately, because they were incomplete at the advent of World War II, none of the portfolios went into the Index. Nonetheless, the vast accumulation of valuable material in the Index, now stored at the National Gallery of Art, Washington, D.C., is a storehouse of information for quilt historians and researchers. This was made possible through the assistance of government sponsorship and gives credence to the importance of funding for similar documentation of contemporary arts.

Inevitably, quilting actually made news in the twentieth century. When Bertha Stenge, the $500 First Prize winner in the 1939–1940 New York World's Fair quilt contest, won a $1,000 Grand Award in the *Woman's Day*'s 1942 contest, the ceremony was broadcast over NBC radio. *Newsweek* magazine covered Mrs. Stenge's 1943 show of thirteen quilts at the Art Institute of Chicago, deemed by the curator "one of the most popular exhibitions the Decorative Arts Department has ever shown."[5] Even in 1944, when all eyes were on the war, *Life* magazine ran a feature describing the making of a "Victory" quilt in Appalachia.[6]

Despite the fervor of the times, quilts made in the period 1900 to 1950 have been largely ignored by collectors and frequently summarily dismissed as being nothing more than "kit quilts," the quilt equivalent of "paint-by-numbers." It is true that a fair number of 1920s, 1930s, and 1940s quilts were made from kits. And those that were not have a good chance of being one of the three most popular patterns—"Double Wedding Ring," "Grandmother's Flower Garden," and "Dresden Plate"—all of which were readily available as commercial patterns. As quilt specialists, we felt that beyond the commonplace lay an unheralded body of work that would confirm the fact that the expert and often ingenious talents of America's quilters flourished in the twentieth century just as they had in the nineteenth. As we began our research, we were delighted to discover not only workmanship that rivals the best of any period in quilting history, but a surprisingly large number of designs completely new to us.

Uncovering the story of quilts from 1900 to 1950 is challenging. Printed matter—articles from dozens of periodicals and hundreds of newspapers—is voluminous and largely uncatalogued. Fortunately, several dedicated quilt historians have begun to research and write about such unwieldy topics as the 800 Nancy Cabot syndicated patterns that appeared in the *Chicago Tribune* during a ten-year period.

Along with the historians, collectors are discovering twentieth-century quilts, partly because fine examples from earlier periods are becoming increasingly rare and expensive. Certainly, then, the time for a new look at this century's quilts has arrived. Quilts from the 1920s have now passed their sixty-fifth birthday and, although not yet antique in the strict 100-year-old sense, are well on their way to becoming respectably collectible. Proof of this lies in the fact that prices for quilts of this period are on the rise. For instance, an extremely fine pictorial quilt from the 1920s, purchased by a collector in New Jersey in 1964 for the then extraordinary sum of $850, recently sold in our gallery for over $6,000. A number of good examples, however, can still be found for under $600.

Compiling a definitive report on the vast numbers of quilts and patterns created between 1900 and 1950 is a task better suited to a computer. Here, we have addressed ourselves to uncovering some of the most remarkable and evocative quilts of the twentieth century and identifying their sources. Although many of these quilts were thought to be original because of their imaginative motifs and superlative workmanship, our research has often shown that they were indeed made with the help of a pattern. Such was the level of pattern design that it is sometimes not easy to distinguish the commercial from the one-of-a-kind.

For the purposes of this book, we will use the term *twentieth century* to denote quilts made between 1900 and 1950. We have avoided entirely the use of the term *Depression quilt*, a misleading phrase coined in recent years. A close look at 1930s quilts shows that there was no one narrowly defined style unique to the Depression period. Certainly, pieced quilts were more popular then, and appliqués were favored in the 1920s; but both decades saw a broad range of styles and creative expression.

In searching out examples for this book, our findings surpassed our most extravagant expectations. Here is evidence that the superior standards of quiltmaking that flourished in the nineteenth century have never left the consciousness of America's needleworkers, and that the tradition of fine workmanship did indeed survive through the years. We hope that the quilts shown on the following pages will lay to rest once and for all the popular idea that quilting in America from 1900 to 1950 was anything less than substantial, distinguished and, at times, wondrous.

7. *Home Arts Needlecraft.* July 1939. A smartly dressed mother and daughter seem to be proof positive that quilting is going modern, as the coverline on this 1939 magazine suggests. While roaming through a needlework bazaar, they have found a "Prince's Feather/Sunburst" quilt to take home. They are passing by a "Star of Bethlehem" quilt and two hooked rugs hanging on the bazaar wall. Photograph courtesy Cuesta Benberry.

# THE GREAT QUILT REVIVAL

What was behind the intense interest in quilting in the 1920s and 1930s? When the twentieth century dawned, quiltmaking was at one of its lowest ebbs. It was exhausted, perhaps, by the gaudy fad for "Crazy" quilts that swept the 1880s and 1890s. The silk and velvet "Crazy" quilt, a decorative bauble, was usually pieced more for show than for warmth or durability. Often it found its way into the parlor, while machine-made blankets and spreads, along with conventional, holdover patchwork, dressed the bed.

Although not all quilters focused on the "Crazy" quilt, even those preferring traditional quilting seemed to have lost their enthusiasm for patchwork by the 1900s. And why not? Manufactured bedding, such as that widely available by mail order from Sears, Roebuck, was eagerly bought. So, too, were the other products of the industrial revolution when they first entered the marketplace. A further discouragement to quilting by hand was provided by the sewing machine, the first appliance that could be purchased on an installment plan. Invented in 1846, it had found its way into even the most rural homes by the early 1900s. And women were delighted. Their sewing chores were dramatically reduced, and they may well have felt that hand quilting was a step backward from the new machine age.

After World War I, however, the mood of the country shifted. The twenties became a period of reappreciating our Colonial American heritage, as well as such "antique" home arts as quilting. Having just rescued Europe in World War I, American patriotism ran high, and so did the feeling that our decorative arts were every bit as worthy as those named after a French Louis or an English George.

In 1923, The American Wing of The Metropolitan Museum of Art opened in New York City. Almost at the same time, Henry Francis du Pont, founder in 1951 of the Winterthur Museum in Delaware, began collecting Americana on a scale only a multimillionaire could afford. By 1928, John D. Rockefeller, Jr., had quietly bought up large quantities of land in what had been Virginia's Colonial capital. That year he announced his intention of restoring Williamsburg and making it "a great center for historical study and inspiration."[7]

Following fast on Rockefeller's heels, Edith Gregor Halpert opened The American Folk Art Gallery in New York City in 1929. An innovation at the time, her gallery proved to be a buying ground for many legendary collectors, including Abby Aldrich Rockefeller, wife of John Jr., whose seminal collection of American folk art later became the nucleus of The Folk Art Center at Williamsburg.

While collecting and launching museums was popular with the very rich, new middle-class suburbanites were moving into Colonial Revival houses, furnished with reproduction Colonial beds, sofas, and secretaries that were advertised in all the magazines. In April 1930, *The House Beautiful* stated that "among the sophisticated, Early American furniture is out of favor because of overuse."[8] That criticism obviously fell on indifferent ears, however, for the Early American look has remained one of the most popular styles of home decorating ever since.

The simple lines of Colonial furniture were particularly welcome in the bedroom. Beds made with ornate wood and yards of drapery were shunned as carriers of disease, as were the layered curtains of the Victorian era. One of the first to give her imprimatur to "our nice Colonial bedrooms"[9] was Elsie de Wolfe, generally considered to be the first professional interior designer. In her book *The House in Good Taste* (1913), she expressed admiration for simple-lined reproduction beds "built for a new service and a new conception of hygiene."[10] Although good taste also borrowed from other periods, especially in other rooms, Miss de Wolfe strongly advocated decorating with simplicity. And she left no doubt in her readers' minds that women should heed her advice. "We may talk of the weather, but we are looking at the furniture," she wrote. "It is a compass that never errs."[11] Clearly, in the twentieth century, a woman's house was to be a reflection of her character.

Along with an urge to decorate simply and make tasteful spreads for Colonial beds, quiltmakers were spurred to new heights by the wonderful fabrics that appeared on the market after World War I. With peace, it was once again possible to import German-made dyes and create clear, bright colors. The dreary, utilitarian fabrics of the war years were soon eclipsed by festive new prints, blossoming with the carefree spirit that characterized the twenties. For quilters, these new prints had a lure beyond their aesthetic quality. By the 1920s, the fabric manufacturing process had been refined so that domestic cottons, long inferior to wools and European cottons, were greatly improved, widely available, and fairly priced. The last period of significant upgrading in cotton-fabric design, during the 1870s and 1880s, had similarly produced a flourish of quiltmaking. In the 1920s, quilters once again eagerly responded to the market's offerings.[12]

Ready to catch one's eyes were cottons in Easter-bright pinks, yellows, and blues and delicate florals with scattered blooms or tiny rosebuds. By the 1930s and early 1940s, these prints became bolder, the colors a little stronger, and the flowers larger and closer together. Motifs like anchors and sailboats reentered fabric design. By the 1950s, rayons and synthetics had become a staple in the marketplace, contributing in part to the subsequent decline of quilting. But prior to the widespread availability of man-made fabrics, the dazzling array of colorful cottons made quilting more attractive than ever.

Although post–World War I fabrics may have inspired quiltmaking, the first glimmerings of the revival can be seen during the war when women were urged to knit socks and, on a smaller scale, to quilt. Some of these patchwork spreads were made to be auctioned off as fund-raisers for the Red Cross, while others were sent to "the orphans in war-torn France and Belgium," or were sewn to use up scraps and "save the blankets for our boys over there," as the 1918 slogans ran.[13] This patriotic call to quilt was swiftly followed by the time-honored urges that drew women to quilting in earlier centuries.

As Carrie Hall wrote in *Romance of the Patchwork Quilt in America* (1935), coauthored with Rose Kretsinger, "when the World War was over and there was no longer a necessity for knitting socks and sweaters, I found my fingers itching for some 'pick-up' work, so I turned to quilt-making, which had always interested me from the time when on my seventh birthday my pioneer mother cut the patches for a star quilt…Quilt-making…not only kept my fingers busy, it stimulated my imagination."[14] A friend of Mrs. Hall concurred, "just to watch the quaint design grow under one's fingers is much more fun than playing bridge."[15]

As with bridge, excelling at patchwork was no simple feat. Quiltmaking required the eye of an artist to arrange the colored bits of fabric in a harmonious and energized composition. A woman's choice of pattern was important, but even a relatively simple "Log Cabin" quilt could, in the hands of one woman, be merely pleasant, while in the hands of another, simply beautiful. Quilting, however, was more than an artistic outlet.

It also satisfied a deep need to be thrifty and industrious, two age-old American virtues especially valued during the Depression. Ironically, although piecing scraps of material seemed frugal, quilts in the twentieth century were not the most practical bedding. Buying batting, thread, fabric for backing, and perhaps a pattern was usually more expensive than purchasing a ready-made blanket. However, a quilt had a strong psychological appeal that no machine-made object could rival.

A quilt was something in which a woman gave of herself—to mark marriages, graduations, and generations as it was handed down from children to grandchildren. In addition, it served as a reminder of her thoughts as she stitched the points of a star just so. It was a fabric diary, pieced with a bit of cloth handed down from her grandmother, or with a scrap from her daughter's christening dress.

A Kansas City man still remembers the powerful role quilts played in his mother's life. When he was young during the Depression, he came home one day and found his mother on the verge of tears, kneeling by her blanket chest. She was distressed because she was going to have to use her mother's quilts, having either too little money or too little time to make her own. She knew that once on the bed they would soon be worn out, so she was grieving in advance for the loss of her mother's treasured legacy.[16]

Quilts in the twentieth century were made to be used, as this story indicates, but only the delight in their creation can explain why many women, given the chance, pieced blanket chests full of quilts, far more than their families could sleep under in a lifetime. Part of this desire to quilt was a creative urge, but certainly a strong factor was the loneliness of rural life.

Much has been written about the farm women of the nineteenth century who sought solace in their piecework and friendship in the much-anticipated quilting bee. Despite the advent of electricity and indoor plumbing, life on the farm was nearly as lonely

8. Scranton, Iowa. May 1940. The generosity of American quilters is demonstrated at this quilting bee, where a Bow Tie quilt is being made for a needy family. Photograph by John Vachon. (Library of Congress)

and isolated in the 1900s as it had been in the mid- to late 1800s. In 1915, 32.4 percent of the American population lived on the farm. By 1935, that figure was not much smaller: 25.3 percent or total of 32,161,000 farm husbands, wives, and children.[17]

The quilting bee still played a social role in rural life, especially during the Depression. As one quilter from Independence, Kansas, pointed out, "we couldn't afford to go anywhere."[18] Grace Snyder, whose quilts are some of the exceptional ones of the era, began to quilt in earnest when, as a young teacher, she was assigned to two pupils on a forlorn Nebraska ranch. Even though she was a twentieth-century woman, the role quilting played in her life was much the same as it had been for her mother and grandmother. Another of the quilters, whose brilliant art is illustrated in this book, is said to have survived the last ten years of her third marriage, during which she was not on speaking terms with her husband, by absorbing herself in quilting.

Loneliness and the need for solace were not limited to the farm in the twentieth century. The city and suburban woman's life was becoming more and more solitary as the new leisure-making appliances offered her an opportunity to run her household without help. Her daughters as well as her sons went away to be educated. And the ice man, the rag man, and the vegetable man who came to her house were becoming a vanishing breed. Her role as mistress of the house was being changed into that of an appliance operator. As a "high-touch" response to such "high-tech" intrusions, quilting was welcome. What better way to exert traditional, protective mothering impulses than by creating bedding that protected loved ones while they slept?

Quilting also found an unexpected niche in the twentieth century as an antidote to the so-called jazz age, and was highly recommended by Carrie Hall and Rose Kretsinger. "We hear so much about this 'jazz age' being hard on the nerves. Quilt-making is the ideal prescription for high-tension nerves. It is soothing," they wrote.[19] Their sentiments were echoed in 1933 in a *Chicago Daily News* article, "Women Are Taking Up Quilting Again," in which writer Ninon observed, "loads of young matrons, even girls, and women who could buy velvet comforters are going in for fine finger sewing along this line...Some probably do so in the long evenings when they formerly went out stepping; or maybe they just feel 'quilty' and it soothes their jagged nerves."[20]

The women who were quilting instead of "stepping" were following an actual medical prescription of Dr. William Dunton, a self-described "physician to nervous ladies," who became interested in quiltmaking and quilt history while seeking cures for his patients. His self-published book, *Old Quilts* (1946), offers his benevolent although sometimes patronizing advice on the subject.

The benefits of home crafts stemmed from the fact that concentration distracts the maker from afflictions both real and imagined. It also helps to develop a more positive attitude. Dr. Dunton, highly respected in the fields of occupational therapy and rehabilitation, credited the spirited competition among quiltmakers

9. Spring cleaning. Coffee County, Alabama. 1939. Rural southern quilters have always taken great pride in their work, regardless of economic status. Scraps and bits of fabrics could be fashioned into colorful patchwork spreads, and sometimes were offered for sale to lucky travelers who happened to take the right country road. Photograph by Marian Post Wolcott. (Library of Congress)

as having beneficial effects and he applauded the community spirit spurred by quilting bees. "Healthy thought" stimulated by quiltmaking was, he felt, a cure for some forms of loneliness. For more seriously disturbed patients in mental hospitals, Dr. Dunton recommended simpler chores such as sorting rags and cutting patterns.[21]

Among matters discussed by the physician were: whether to use the term *The American Peasant Art*[22]— he felt it was not appropriate since he believed wealthy homes were where America's first quilts appeared; and the availability in stores of printed patchwork, "an old trick" dating back at least to the 1850s, under the trade name Challie de Mousseline. Regarding the latter, he pointed out the wide variation in the quality of color harmony, suggesting that "modern color printing is akin to blowing a French horn, in that one knows what goes in but what comes out is most uncertain."[23] He also acknowledged the renewal of interest in *trapunto*, a term used to describe white quilts with elaborate designs created with stuffed and corded work.

His writing on the subject of quilting remains an important documentation for quilt historians. In addition to his contributions regarding contemporary quilting, his study of "Baltimore Album" quilts remained the most comprehensive nearly four decades later, when the subject was expanded definitively by Dena Katzenberg of the Baltimore Museum of Art.

# A FOLK ART GROWS UP

Quilts made in American homes in the nineteenth century, with the possible exception of the "Crazy" quilt, are considered folk art. In the twentieth century the *folk* element was in danger of being swiftly swept away by the commercial marketplace and the media. But the *art* remained much as it had been, surprisingly untouched by the industrial revolution. Women still pieced and appliquéd their quilt tops by hand, leaving the sewing machine idle in the corner, except, perhaps, when they needed to sew on a binding, which was more durable if done by machine. Occasionally, certain quilters would speed their work with machine piecing, particularly if they were making simple, straight-lined patterns such as the various "Log Cabin" designs. The Amish usually pieced their quilts by a treadle-driven machine. But by and large, bending over the machine with its whirring motor seemed much more like work than sitting in a comfortable chair sewing. And quilting in the twentieth century was primarily a leisure activity. The quilting bee, always a much-anticipated social activity celebrating the craft of hand quilting, never was seriously threatened by the advent of the sewing machine. A group of friends gathered to quilt was a perfect setting for exchanging news and gossip, and it was the ultimate showcase for needle artistry. If a woman did not have a network of friends to gather for a quilting bee, and if she was not inclined to do the work herself, she simply sent her top out to a professional to be quilted.

Although quilting remained a handmade art, almost everything else about it changed dramatically in the twentieth century. Pattern exchange, for example, was no longer something personal that transpired only among family and friends, sometimes with handmade scrapbooks. Designs became part of the commercial marketplace. One catalogue contained more patterns than a mid-nineteenth-century quilter might have seen in all her life. And once they were bought and sold through catalogues, magazines, and syndicated newspaper columns, they lost much of their regional character. Quilting became a homogenized, national craft. Even some of the Amish quilters made "worldly" patterns, such as the Ladies Art Company's "Fanny's Fan" in their own preferred solid colors, of course.

Another new development in the twentieth century was the growing number of professional quilt designers. As early as 1905, *The Ladies' Home Journal*, one of the most successful of the healthy crop of women's periodicals, asked leading artists such as Maxfield Parrish and Jessie Willcox Smith and writers such as Ernest Thompson Seton, a founder of the Boy Scouts, to create motifs for quilts. Although it is doubtful that these patterns were ever translated into quilts—they were created with little regard for the requirements of the stitched medium—*The Ladies' Home Journal* showed considerable imagination in publishing these fascinating original designs. It would be fun to see what our own contemporary artists, such as Julian Schnabel, or even entertainment superstars like Michael Jackson, might create to challenge quilters.

*The Ladies' Home Journal* series signaled the new way that the twentieth century was looking at quilts— as art. Patterns had become something that could be professionally designed. Indeed, in the thirties, newspapers such as the *Kansas City Star* and syndicated pattern columns like "Aunt Martha" featured the work of professional artists who often knew little of quilting but could meet the insatiable demand for new patterns.[24]

Often, too, prominent experts in the field had a fine-arts background. Rose Kretsinger, coauthor of *The Romance of the Patchwork Quilt in America*, attended and taught at the Art Institute of Chicago. She toured Europe and designed jewelry before taking up quiltmaking in her forties. Her sophisticated background is reflected in the curvilinear quality of some of her designs, inspired by the Art Nouveau style. Ruby McKim, a graduate of The Parson's School of Design in New York City, who operated her own syndicated pattern company, had been the youngest art superintendent of the Kansas City schools. Her patterns show a very sophisticated, Art Deco–like quality, echoing contemporary design trends.

Until the twentieth century, quilt design was something that occurred from the bottom up: a woman with a beautiful pattern would often lend it to her neighbors, and so it might well travel throughout several communities. With the advent of strong media interest in quilting, the situation was reversed. Needlework editors offered a number of new designs that women could imitate or buy patterns for. Anne Orr, for example, who was on the staff of *Good Housekeeping* from 1919 to 1940 created one of the most distinctive pattern styles. Her quilts almost look like computer graphics, with tiny squares and blocks of subtly graded color, which were her translation of cross-stitch into quilting (figs. 35, 36). Anne Orr was also a prime example of a new kind of quilter that prospered in the twentieth century: the entrepreneur. To meet the demand for her quilt designs, she went into business selling patterns, iron-on transfers, and quilt kits from her studio in Nashville, Tennessee. She employed over 160 women in the course of her career and, in addition, had 60 women in Kentucky sewing quilts in her designs for customers who chose not to make their own.

The immediate recognition that talented quilters received offered other enterprising women unexpected career opportunities. Lillian Walker, for example, born in 1870 in Middletown, Iowa, first became known for her designs when she won two dollars sometime in the 1920s for the best quilt on a clothesline in a contest sponsored by pattern-company owner Carlie Sexton Holmes, of Wheaton, Illinois. Mrs. Walker then sent some of her quilts off to a show in Illinois and immediately received a dozen orders. Soon she had hired ten women to baste tops and ten more to do the actual quilting, and found herself with a thriving business.[25]

Other career possibilities came from the lecture circuit. Carrie Hall, coauthor of *The Romance of the Patchwork Quilt in America*, used to dress in a Colonial costume of red moiré, trimmed with a frilled net fichu (an old-fashioned triangular scarf), and lecture in department stores and to ladies' groups, illustrating her talk with quilt blocks from her collection.

Mrs. Hall, her costume aside, was an example of another new development in the twentieth century: the quilt historian. Mrs. Hall began collecting quilt blocks after World War I to preserve and document the vast number of patterns she came across. She made over 1,000 by hand and sketched even more. Her magnificent collection of 800 blocks was donated to the Spencer Museum of Art, University of Kansas in Lawrence, and can be studied there by appointment.

Another quilt historian, Betty Harned Harriman (1890–1971), born in Bunceton, Missouri, became interested in old quilts while living in Virginia. She asked permission to sketch and photograph spreads on beds in many of the state's important old homes and house museums. Thus inspired, she began collecting antique fabrics and quilts and eventually reproduced famous quilts using historic fabrics to preserve the designs.[26]

Quilt-book author Florence Peto (1884–1970) also reproduced antique quilts using swatches of textiles such as William Penn's grandson's drapery. Her interest in quilting, however, was primarily oriented toward documenting the often-forgotten individual makers. She lectured widely on the East Coast and, through her New York City radio broadcast for the WPA's Index of American Design, she encouraged more people to lend their quilts to the project for rendering. Her research revealed that many "new" techniques, such as lap quilting, were actually early and forgotten methods of quilting.

The twentieth century was also the first era when books solely devoted to quilting were published; the landmark volume being Marie D. Webster's *Quilts: Their Story and How to Make Them* (1915), which included color plates of quilts she had designed while she was needlework editor at *The Ladies' Home Journal*. Her research began in Egypt, worked its way up through the Middle Ages and Old England, and finally concluded with the history of quilting in America. This study of a simple patchwork spread as an item with a significant history and design legacy was a great achievement.

Webster's book was followed by Ruth Finley's *Old Patchwork Quilts* in 1929, which covered the making of quilts, the origins of quilt names, and even the migration of patterns. Truly ground-breaking was Carrie Hall and Rose Kretsinger's *Romance of the Patchwork Quilt in America* (1933), which contained Mrs. Hall's 800 different quilt blocks, a source for pattern identification that remains invaluable. Florence Peto further filled in the quilt picture with *Historic Quilts* in 1939 and *American Quilts and Coverlets* in 1949. In between these came Dr. William Rush Dunton's *Old Quilts* in 1946, which offered his theory that quilting was excellent occupational therapy for "nervous ladies" and which impressively documented the "Baltimore Album" quilt, as previously mentioned.

Other important books include Elizabeth Wells Robertson's *American Quilts* (c. 1948) and Marguerite Ickis's *The Standard Book of Quiltmaking and Collecting* (1949). In recognition of their outstanding work, four of these authors, Finley, Ickis, Peto, and Dunton, have been recently elected to the Quilters Hall of Fame by the Continental Quilting Congress, a publicly funded quilt-study organization.

# DESIGN SOURCES

It has been suggested that quilt patterns were more derivative in the twentieth century than in previous eras. In a certain sense it is true that women approached quilting as an "antique" home art. As with furniture, they were looking for reproductions. One of the favorite quilt patterns sold by Mrs. Scioto Danner, a widely successful mail-order pattern source, was "The Ladies' Dream," which had been copied from a quilt that had been in Mrs. W. L. Harbison's family for six generations. No one else was ever granted permission to copy it. With that sort of pedigree, pattern buyers naturally snapped up "The Ladies' Dream."

Even one of the most creative sources of quilt design—the Century of Progress competition sponsored by Sears, Roebuck in honor of the Chicago exposition in 1933—showed favoritism toward traditional design. The Grand Prize of $1,000 was to be supplemented by $200 if the winning quilt reflected the Century of Progress theme. The $200 bonus motivated many women to invent unique designs. Louise Rowley of Chicago stitched a bird's-eye view of the fairgrounds. Mrs. W. B. Lathouse of Ohio illustrated the idea of progress with a wringer washing machine, a table radio, and a refrigerator, all of which surrounded a portrait of President Franklin Delano Roosevelt (fig. 147). The Chicago fire, Fort Dearborn, and the city's architecture inspired other quilts, but the judges never awarded the $200 bonus. Instead, the Grand Prize went to a traditional star enhanced with very fine quilting. It seems that virtuoso quilting was what the judges most admired, even more than color and composition and much more than originality of design.[27]

Like the judges of the Century of Progress competition, American women were exceedingly interested in patterns from the past. In terms of the commercial marketplace, this led to a great deal of valuable research. The first two pattern catalogues, those published by the Ladies Art Company in 1898 and by Clara Stone in 1910, were devoted almost entirely to traditional designs from the nineteenth century and are welcome references today. Their research provided the foundation for many of the pattern catalogues that were to follow.

The issue of derivation is even more complicated, because in tracing the origins of most quilt patterns, one is led on a circuitous route back to antiquity. Many twentieth-century patterns, linked back to the nineteenth century, can be found to have been inspired by such objects as an Oriental rug, an Indian palampore, or a glazed chintz brought to America from the Orient or from Europe. The "Variable Star" pattern, one of the most pleasing of pieced-quilt designs, can be seen in the stained glass of a window by Laurentius Cosma in the thirteenth-century Church of Santa Maria in Ara Coeli, Rome.[28] The "Irish Chain" pattern, long a favorite among American quilters, is remarkably similar to an early nineteenth-century drawing of a Persian pavement by Mirza Akbar, now in the Victoria & Albert Museum in London.[29]

Furthermore, some of the most remarkable quilts made in the twentieth century are those inspired by magnificent designs from the past. Pine Eisfeller's tour-de-force appliqué spread (fig. 41) was adapted from an elaborate decorative motif on a seventeenth-century Persian linen carpet, now at the Victoria & Albert Museum in London. Also, Charlotte Jane Whitehill used "Cherry Trees and Robins," an 1820 appliqué quilt, as the inspiration for her superb "Cherry Tree" quilt (1936; fig. 181). The "Paradise Garden" by Rose Kretsinger (frontispiece, page ii) is a magnificent twentieth-century reworking of a nineteenth-century floral appliqué.

An outstanding reinterpretation of a past motif that also offers a fascinating glimpse of the way quilt patterns travel through history is a "Pot of Flowers" appliqué quilt (fig. 58). Our interest in its history was sparked because our 1930s version had such superb design and stitchery that it seemed to be of another era. Yet the fabrics used were unmistakably made in the twentieth century. The machinelike accuracy of the pattern and its application made us wonder if perhaps our "Pot of Flowers" had been made from a commercial design. Further investigation uncovered a number of other quilts, which, although they contained minor variations reflecting their different makers, bore an uncanny resemblance to our quilt.

The earliest possible antecedent to our quilt was Rose Kretsinger's very similar "Pride of Iowa," made sometime between 1925 and 1934, which she credits to a nineteenth-century pattern. Her interpretation included a graceful feather appliqué border, which was more traditional than the key border in the Art Deco style on our "Pot of Flowers." Searching further, we found a 1931 "Michigan Flower Pot" made by Metta McRoberts Pearl of Oberlin, Ohio. "Potted Tulip," by Mrs. G. M. Forney of Thurman, Iowa, appeared in the September 1929 issue of *Farm and Fireside* as a prizewinner in the magazine's own quilt contest. One among over 1,000 entries, this variation of our quilt tied for third place. Its pattern was offered as #FC-237 and could be ordered from the magazine for twenty-five cents. The magazine noted that an advantage to this quilt pattern was that its top was made of only four units, each measuring 34 inches square. These were then appliquéd with twenty-seven different pieces. A single block, it was suggested, would make a fine wall hanging.

We had indeed found a pattern in the history of our quilt, but on what was it based? Delving back still further, we uncovered "Caroline's Quilt," made by Caroline Charlotta Greiner of Blaine, Ohio, around 1910, which shows the same floral motif done a little more sparsely, particularly in the border.[30] We discovered an antecedent to this quilt, a small, pristine spread of around 1860 made for a crib, at Historic Deerfield in Massachusetts. In this version, the border had pieced triangles with alternating red and white patches and the appliqué work was more elaborate, with stuffed berries and extraordinary quilting. A full-size version of this quilt, done about the same time, is in the Mary Barton collection in Iowa.

Finally, we found the earliest version of this motif at the Shelburne Museum in Vermont. Thought to have been made in 1830, it is called "Little Birds."[31] The source of this rendition could have been an antique vase, printed textile, oil painting, or a detail from an old household decorative object.

In the twentieth century, interpretations of this motif have appeared in every decade: Charlotte Jane Whitehill, a well-known quilter, made a version after ours in 1940, calling it "Our Pride," which is now in The Denver Art Museum. Recently, the same pattern emerged in a contemporary spread displayed at the Living History Farms in Des Moines, Iowa, as a raffle prize.

How did the quilters all come to use the same motif, even though they lived in different states and quilted over a period of more than a hundred years? Prior to the pattern's publication in 1929, it would be safe to say that it somehow traveled from person to person, a faraway visit affording a glimpse of one version of the quilt that was either copied or stored away in a quilter's memory. We have seen many instances where patterns were thought to be original, even by the maker, when actually they were re-created from a dim memory, much as a songwriter sincerely believes he has originated a tune, only to find out that it is simply a rediscovery of an old song.

In addition to such fascinating reworkings of past patterns, the twentieth century produced a vast number of new designs in record-breaking volume, a response to the need to publish new material in the newspaper and magazine columns. In conception, these designs are not very different from those of the nineteenth century in that they reflect the quilter's or the designer's environment. The difference is that, in addition to looking to nature for "Turkey Tracks," "Rising Sun," and other patterns, they were also inspired by coffee cups, airplanes (figs. 69, 70), and even images from the daily comics (fig. 186). Events such as Arizona's entry into the Union in 1912 inspired quilters. One *Kansas City Star* needlework editor came back from the zoo with an idea for an "Elephant" pattern that she drew up for her quilt column. Readers complained that she might be politically biased, so the following week she published a "Donkey" design.[32]

Some of the most powerful inspirations came from personal experience, such as Bertha Stenge's splendid "Quilt Show" (fig. 174), in which each square portrays a woman holding a quilt of a different design. Just as personal is Fannie Shaw's "Prosperity Is Just Around the Corner" (p. v), illustrated with her neighbors—the butcher, the farmer, the teacher, the housewife, etc.—each looking for the fulfillment of Herbert Hoover's promise.

The idea of drawing on one's environment was recommended by Elizabeth King, writing on the appliqué technique in 1934.[33] She suggested training the eye to discern potential quilt designs in unaccustomed places: a flock of flying geese, a squadron of airplanes, or even the patterns in wallpaper. One famous quilter who agreed with this approach was Rose Kretsinger, whose "Orchid Wreath" was inspired by a Coca-Cola poster. Mrs. Kretsinger also borrowed ideas from pieces of old quilts that had survived the 1871 Chicago fire, as well as from motifs in books.

A contemporary illustration of this design process comes from Mary Leman, daughter-in-law of Bonnie Leman, founder and editor-in-chief of *Quilter's Newsletter Magazine*. She chose the intricate handknit pattern of a Shetland wool-lace shawl as a source for a charming quilt-stitchery design. To create the straight lines, she used a ruler; for the curves, a saucer or plate. Similarly, out-of-the-ordinary sources, such as gravestones and manhole-cover rubbings and the tile floor of a luncheonette provided further sources of creativity.[34]

In the first half of the twentieth century, much new decorative-arts material was being published. The subjects of books in this field ranged from Japanese design to mosaic floors in early churches of Palestine. All of these provided inspiration for quilting, as did the discovery of Tutankhamen's tomb in Egypt in 1922. Its treasures sparked a fascination with all things Egyptian, which proved an especially appropriate influence for patchwork. As early as 1960 B.C., the Egyptians had been practicing patchwork, as seen in a canopy made for a queen. Egyptian art, with its flat planes of harmonious colors and striking angles, could be well adapted to one-dimensional quilt design. Large appliquéd floral motifs show this influence, as well as the outlining of details with black.

Art Nouveau, Art Deco, and the changing design styles of the twentieth century were not without their influence on quilting. Although the distance between Peoria and Paris has always been considerable, it grew less so in the 1900s. Expositions, exhibitions, and fairs such as the Century of Progress, held in Chicago in 1933, and similar ones abroad, were frequented by American manufacturers and artists, who brought decorative-arts ideas to products and advertising. The national magazines, for the most part guided by knowledgeable New York editors, helped spread design news, as did the department stores.

In the twentieth century, department stores played a unique role as meccas of sophistication. Even in small towns in the Midwest, it was not unusual for women to drive or take trains to urban centers like Kansas City to shop at the department stores. In addition to the glamour of the latest fashions, the stores frequently featured quilt displays, often from Mountain Mist, Mrs. Danner, and other pattern sources. It was probably natural, therefore, that a cross-pollination would occur and the influence of the Art Nouveau and Art Deco styles would appear in quilts.

Art Nouveau preached that nature was "the infallible code of all laws of beauty."[35] Although Art Nouveau peaked in popularity around 1900 and faded from fashion around World War I, untold numbers of quilts from 1900 to 1950 were horticulturally inspired. As a source for flower and leaf designs, many quilters turned to farm almanacs, horticultural journals, and books. Some interpreted nature literally, but others caught the spirit of Art Nouveau artists who "wished to explore the forces of growth and represent them symbolically,"[36] translating exotic plants and tendrils of vines into sinuous appliqué. As the preferred medium for quilting in the 1920s, appliqué was especially suited to adapting curvaceous Art Nouveau motifs.

One quilter who made very beautiful quilts in the Art Nouveau style was Hannah Haynes Headlee. Born in Topeka, Kansas, in 1866, Mrs. Headlee grew up with an interest in painting. Then in 1914, she traveled to New York and served as a chaperone while her niece attended the New York School of Fine and Applied Arts. Her exposure to the latest art ideas is seen in her quilts using iris (fig. 52), a peacock (fig. 182), flowing water (fig. 183), and other popular Art Nouveau motifs.

The angular, stylized, and streamlined aesthetic of Art Deco, popular from 1918 to 1939, was perhaps even more adaptable to patchwork. Pieced quilts, fragmented and geometric, were abstracted, almost cubist works, developed well before the age of Picasso. Pattern designer Ruby McKim, owner of the influential McKim Studios, captured the Art Deco spirit in her stylized flower quilts. Her *Designs Worth Doing* features jauntily "Moderne" patchwork patterns for an airplane and butterfly. It is her "Oriental Poppy" quilt (fig. 59), however, in which flowers dance with the energy of the Charleston, that seems most typical of the Deco age that gave birth to such masterworks as Radio City Music Hall in New York City and the sleek *Normandie* ocean liner.

Although the influence of changing trends in art and design was relatively new to quilting, politics was a time-honored inspiration for quilters. A patriotic emblem like the American eagle appeared in patchwork almost as soon as it was adopted by Congress in 1782 as part of the Great Seal of the United States. In the twentieth century, patriotic motifs continued to be translated into quilting. In the thirties, a stylized blue eagle was the unmistakable symbol of the NRA (National Recovery Act), part of Franklin Roosevelt's New Deal. Consequently, Nancy Cabot, a pattern syndicate, adapted the NRA symbol for its "Blue

10. Art Nouveau motif appliqué. Ca. 1900. 96" x 78". Tracking down sources for quilt designs is an endless and fascinating challenge. These curvaceous, almost flame-shape flowers are typically Art Nouveau. Interestingly, they have been repeated simply as single images, without other lavishly interlaced organic shapes, in a manner befitting the humble quilt tradition. (Collection of Joanna S. Rose)

11. Perhaps the ultimate kit quilt, the Paragon Pattern Company of New York offered this pattern as American Glory #01147. The company stated that this popular pattern was based on an antique quilt in the Titus Geesey Collection at the Philadelphia Museum of Art. A number of mid-twentieth-century examples made from the kit exist and are frequently mistaken for nineteenth-century spreads.

Eagle," which, despite its lofty name, some observers thought rather resembled an army of frogs.

When FDR became president, Ruth Finley designed "The Roosevelt Rose," a scallop-edged appliqué spread offered as a pattern by *Good Housekeeping* for twenty-five cents in its January 1934 issue. A quilt made to honor both Franklin and Eleanor, "The Rose of the Field," appeared in the August 1933 issue of *Needlecraft* magazine. In addition to blocks with field roses, it had a top border of five buds—one for each of the Roosevelt children. FDR's inaugural speech, "Freedom from Want, Freedom from War . . . ," inspired Bertha Stenge to design a commemorative quilt and a pattern offered by *Woman's Day* magazine in the 1940s. For those interested in Roosevelt and the other twenty-nine presidents the W.L.M. Clark Co. of St. Louis offered a set ($1.00 postpaid) of stamped blocks with the portraits of Washington through Hoover, plus an eighteen-inch center-medallion square featuring Roosevelt. These blocks, intended to be embroidered, could be alternated with plain blocks for an extra four cents each. Incidentally, quilt-pattern makers attempted to cover all bases. Alfred M. Landon, FDR's Republican opponent in 1936, was honored with "Landon's Sunflower," thereby saluting both Mr. Landon and his native state, Kansas, through its official flower.

The swastika, an ancient Greek motif dishonored in its reversed form by the horrors of Nazi Germany, was a frequent pattern prior to Hitler.[37] At that time, the design was simply another patchwork motif akin to "Flyfoot" or "Bow Knot." Ancient Indian artifacts such as pottery and the more recent "winter count" hides, as well as woven blankets, sometimes contain the motif, indicating its universality as a symbol in human consciousness. Its true origins in antiquity, are, unfortunately, overshadowed by its sinister twentieth-century symbolism. Even though pre–World War II quilters could not have foreseen its use by Hitler, it is difficult now not to be somewhat startled at coming across it in patchwork.

When World War II arrived, it inspired a wide range of quilts. *The Ladies' Home Journal* offered the "War Bride's Quilt" and the "Navy Wives Quilt," which had Navy insignia. The magazine suggested that the latter would be a useful group project. Many quilts were made during World Wars I and II to auction as fundraisers for the Red Cross and other organizations. Two servicemen abroad created "The Army Star" for the *Kansas City Star* newspaper. Mountain Mist's offerings included "Sea Wings to Glory," still sold today.[38]

Of course, the most powerful of the war motifs was the V symbol, liberally employed on "Victory" quilts. A 1944 "Victory" quilt made by two Appalachian

12. Red Cross project. Ca. 1917. The Red Cross sponsored sewing projects, such as this one undertaken by a group of dedicated young ladies in St. Paul, Minnesota, which contributed to the war effort. A stack of patchwork spreads is proudly displayed along with cotton potholders—made like miniature, knotted comforters—all items well suited to fundraising by community organizations. Photograph courtesy Minnesota Historical Society.

women, America Hatfield and Rhoda McCoy, commemorated their loved ones lost or serving in the war, as well as the founders of their clans. When it was finished at a quilting bee, their neighbors composed a ballad in celebration and *Life* magazine ran a story on it.[39] Widely circulated magazines and pattern syndicates, such as Aunt Martha and Nancy Page, all offered "Victory" designs.

In addition to these pattern innovations, the twentieth century also saw a number of old patterns revived and renamed, which adds a considerable challenge to tracing their origins. When, on January 7, 1928, Mayor Jimmy Walker of New York City talked by telephone with Sir Roland Blandes, Lord Mayor of London, thus inaugurating the first Atlantic telegraph cable line, the "Rope" quilting pattern was instantly rechristened "Cable." With Teddy Roosevelt's presidency, "Swing in the Center" became "Mrs. Roosevelt's Favorite." The desire to make old patterns seem up-to-date accounts for some of the name changes. A more common motivation, however, was that magazines and newspapers wanted to make a pattern seem new when they republished it. One example that illustrates the many renamings possible is "Double Wrench," researched by Cuesta Benberry. First published with that title in 1884 by the periodical *Farm and Fireside*, it appeared in various publications from 1900 to 1919 as "Square Triangle," "Maltese

Cross," and "Bride's Knot." By the 1920s, it had become "Aeroplane," "T Design," and "Fisherman's Reel," among others. In the 1930s, its names included "Baseball Diamond" and even "Colonial Design."[40] Although "name games" did not always meet with the approval of quilters—at times the custom was sharply criticized in irate letters to magazine editors—pattern recycling flourished.

Despite these illustrations of liberal reuse of material, there was some concern about copying in the first half of the twentieth century. Hawaiian quilters always felt it was very bad luck to borrow another's design, since their motifs were believed to have sprung from a very personal vision belonging exclusively to the quiltmaker. Copyright laws, however, were generally not considered to apply to quilt designs in the period 1900 to 1950. Some worried, however, whether a pattern printed by a magazine would be covered by its copyright. For that reason, Aunt Martha, a syndicated pattern company, was always careful to have its staff artists alter a design slightly if they were "borrowing" it from another source.[41]

# WORLDLY THINGS

Two of the most distinctive types of American quilts, each very different from the other, have come from the Amish and the Hawaiians. In the twentieth century, these two areas of regional creativity influenced the quilt designs of "outsiders" while remaining relatively unchanged themselves.

Interestingly, both groups were latecomers to the quilting tradition. Almost all Amish quilts are dated after 1860. It has been suggested that Amish bishops might have forbidden piecing of quilts or that women simply wove blankets prior to that time. The tradition of Amish quilts, which flourished extraordinarily from 1870 to 1935, seems to have been borrowed from the "English" neighbors of the Amish.

Although both the midwestern and the Pennsylvania Amish quilts saw little design change from the nineteenth to the twentieth centuries, some hallmarks of twentieth-century quilting did appear in their spreads. In the nineteenth century and then during World War I, the Amish generally dyed most of their wools for quilts, but in the 1920s they began to buy their fabrics at stores and soon switched to the wool crepes and cottons that were widely available. Although a plain backing was preferred, sometimes these quilts were backed with a plaid or a flowered flannel, the patterns evidently being considered acceptable because they were hidden most of the time.

When synthetic battings and fabrics such as rayon came on the market in the late 1930s, 1940s, and 1950s, the Amish were eager purchasers because their quilts were much more durable if they were made with the synthetics. Unfortunately, however, these modern developments caused a decline in the high level of workmanship in Amish quilts. Synthetic battings, though easier to run a needle through, were much thicker and therefore dramatically reduced the number of possible quilting stitches per inch. Also, the rayons and blends were more slippery and thus not conducive to fine needlework. Finally, in the forties, the colors of Amish quilts began to change. Quilters began to abandon the lustrous dark backgrounds in favor of the more conventional materials available. Today the Amish view the dark quilts as old-fashioned, which is one reason why they have been willing to sell their vintage quilts to dealers and collectors avidly seeking minimal art for their walls. The finely quilted, distinctive patterns have virtually disappeared in modern Amish quilts, rendering them indistinguishable from other contemporary spreads.

Like the Amish, the Hawaiian quilters departed from the American quilting tradition in that they seldom used print fabrics, relying instead on graphic combinations of two colors, frequently red against white, but also orange, blue, purple, and green on white. The tradition of piecing scraps of material was originally alien to the Hawaiians, whose clothing was tied instead of being cut and fitted, the process that produces leftover scraps. Thus, when the missionaries began to teach quilting to the native women around the 1830s, the Hawaiians used a large piece of fabric from which to cut their appliqué patterns and quickly developed their own unique aesthetic. Their imaginative patterns, cut from folded tapa (woven fiber) or paper the way children make snowflakes, resemble the abstract block-printed motifs that decorated the tapa bedcovers the quilts replaced.

Although Hawaiian quilting was first done at quilting bees, as taught by the missionary ladies, the work soon became the task of the individual, partly to keep the stitching uniform. The Hawaiians were also very protective of their designs. Only the closest of friends exchanged patterns, and a quilter was wary of having her design "lifted," perhaps while her quilt was sunning on the line, before her work was completed. To steal a pattern, it was believed, was to steal something of the owner's soul or power. It is only in recent years that Hawaiian quilt exhibitions and a general sharing of patterns have occurred.

One twentieth-century quilter who was very influenced by Hawaiian quilts and helped bring attention to them was Pine Hawkes Eisfeller. In 1930, she and her husband, Robert, who was in the Army Medical Corps, were sent to Hawaii. As she wrote in *American Home* in 1945: "One day I was asked if I had ever seen any Hawaiian quilts. I hadn't and from the descriptions, I was unable to picture them in my mind. But I inquired among my friends and eventually found a woman who knew a woman who owned one . . ." After that, she discovered a Hawaiian quilt shop that she would frequent with a sketchbook, much to the disapproval of the owner. Mrs. Eisfeller then began creating her own quilts based on the Hawaiian designs she had seen and selling tops to the Army wives for $10. She could do two a day.[42]

In 1935, she moved back to Oswego, New York, and entered her quilts in the Syracuse State Fair, winning two first and two second prizes. In 1942, she won the second Grand Award and second prize in the Outline Class and a first in the Quilting Class in a *Woman's Day* contest, surpassing Rose Kretsinger and Bertha Stenge in the Quilting category. She also created Hawaiian patterns for the Rock River Cotton Company and lectured on Hawaiian quilting to women's clubs.[43]

# PATTERNS FOR SALE

One of the most misunderstood aspects of the twentieth-century quilt revival is the significant role played by commercial enterprises that published catalogues, patterns, and kits. The mere suggestion that a quilt might be made from or inspired by a commercial design has, for some, cast a pall on the work, as if this eliminated all possibility of originality, quality, and importance. Of course, a number of the mass-marketed patterns and kits were strictly mundane. Yet a good many of them were the inspired contributions of both talented housewives who sent their patterns to magazines and famous needlework designers who were enterprising enough to share their artistry. The best of these patterns remain as a valuable historical record documenting a highly creative period in quiltmaking.

The fact that some of these patterns were used by newspapers and magazines as enticements for subscribers or that they were distributed by the new mail-order entrepreneurs for a profit should not discredit the fine quilters who used them. Today, we tend to value original designs above all else, but quilters in the 1920s and 1930s were less concerned with a pattern's uniqueness and were more interested in being able to complete a difficult quilt skillfully. For example, in the early thirties, Anna Chaney, a quilter in Bowling Green, Kentucky, made a sateen quilt with a plume pattern. Her friends admired it so much that two or three of them traced the design and made their own versions. When Mrs. Chaney let it be known that she was sending her quilt to a Sears, Roebuck contest in Louisville, her friends also sent their plume quilts in—and all won honorable mention![44]

Just as many a sewer today would never dream of making a dress without buying a pattern from Butterick or McCall's, quilters in the early twentieth century considered a pattern a natural prerequisite to cutting out a quilt. With this as a guide, they were able to lay out and complete complicated spreads. And they gained access to an abundance of sophisticated designs that otherwise might not have reached their communities.

The idea of providing quilters with step-by-step diagrams and foolproof instructions was far from new. Quilting "how-tos" had been published throughout the second half of the nineteenth century, particularly during the "Crazy"-quilt period, when women were eager for guidance in embroidering their silk and velvet patchworks. One design for a "Center Medallion" quilt published by *Cassell's Illustrated Family Paper* on May 13, 1865, included an admonition that quilters should avoid "unsightly and comparatively valueless" results by following their format as exactly as possible.[45]

Although using patterns was nothing new, an industry to produce and promote them was. A commercial development that marked the demise of the neighborly origins of patterns, this industry did have several interesting hallmarks. One was that the

13, 14, 15. Appliqué basket quilt center made by Elizabeth Harriman, early 1920s, Bunceton, Missouri. 40½" x 30½". Cotton sateen. An iron-on transfer pattern # 1187, costing 40¢ from McCall was the design source for this cheerful quilt center. As the instructions suggested, she made a tracing on the tissue-paper pattern before ironing so that she could use it to cut additional blooms. Note that she added a lavish ribbon bow from another pattern to her basket. Photograph courtesy Cuesta Benberry. (Collection of Mary Schafer, Flushing, Michigan)

search for patterns to be published led to a tremendous amount of research into nineteenth-century designs. The innovator in this research was the Ladies Art Company of St. Louis, Missouri, which published its *Diagrams of Quilt, Sofa and Pin Cushion Patterns* in 1898. Its collection of 420 design blocks for piecework, except for two pages of appliqué designs, are an invaluable reference today.

The Ladies Art Company began largely as a family operation. Paper pattern pieces were cut out by hand, folded, and tucked into an envelope on which the design number was written. When the children came home from school, they would watercolor the card showing the completed block. By 1922, Ladies Art had fifty people working in a plant, designing patterns, stamping cloth for kits, producing instruction pamphlets on a wide range of needle arts, operating mimeograph machines, and processing mail orders. It prospered until World War II, when a shortage of paper, lack of available employees, and a declining demand curtailed its business.

The Ladies Art Company's first competitor emerged around 1910 when New Englander Clara Stone published *Practical Needlework Patterns* with the C.W. Caulkins Co. of Boston, Massachusetts. Her 186 traditional patterns were largely an outgrowth of her vast contributions to *Hearth & Home*'s pattern column. Both her research and that of the Ladies Art Company provided a core of historical material upon which later firms liberally drew.

As the century progressed, another development appeared in the pattern industry: the designer. Marie Webster, *The Ladies' Home Journal*'s needlework editor from 1911 to 1917, led the way with her pattern business of the early 1920s, operated from her home in Marion, Indiana. Mrs. Webster's touch was felt not just in her superlative designs, which were largely appliqué, but also in the correspondence with her customers. When Ruth Snyder of Independence, Kansas, ordered an appliqué pattern for a "Morning Glory" quilt, she asked for help with the actual quilting design, so Mrs. Webster sketched one right on the tissue-paper pattern.[46]

Other talented quilt designers with a flair for business included Carlie Sexton Holmes, a contributor to *Better Homes & Gardens* as well as a number of farm journals, who ran a pattern business from Des Moines, Iowa. She also sponsored a contest for the best photograph of a quilt on a clothesline and published the results in a twelve-page pamphlet in 1928. Anne Orr, *Good Housekeeping*'s Art-Needlework Editor from 1919 to 1940, ran an extensive pattern and kit business from Nashville, Tennessee, and also designed booklets of patterns published under her name for Montgomery Ward and Lockport Batting. The popularity of her patterns was astounding: on a single day in 1917, she is said to have received 500,000 requests for her own brochures. Rose Kretsinger, coauthor of *The Romance of the Patchwork Quilt in America*, freely shared her patterns for years, but finally she, too, began selling them for $2.00 to $3.50 each.

While the number of players in the pattern business was growing, it still could be a very simple operation, run with a very low overhead, as the story of Mrs. Scioto Danner of El Dorado, Kansas, illustrates. When Mrs. Danner realized that selling a quilt, which could bring $25.00 around 1930, was "like finding an oil well," she arranged to have her quilts displayed at the Innes department store in Wichita, Kansas. Many women, unable to afford a finished quilt, inquired about her patterns. How to produce them? The department-store manager suggested a solution: have the girls in the business department of the local high school cut the stencils and mimeograph them on white, legal-size paper. That proved to be Mrs. Danner's method of "manufacture" right through the 1950s. A bookcase in her home served as her "warehouse." Her patterns sold for twenty-five cents to $2.00, the cheapest ones being for piecework. She found these especially popular in frugal New England, partly because women there considered pieced quilts more "historic." But in the rest of the country, Mrs. Danner discovered, "people bought the pattern for the quilt they admired most, regardless of the price."[47]

As Mrs. Danner's story shows, the pattern business thrived because of tremendous demand. When a woman's quilt was displayed at a store or awarded a prize, be it the Grand Prize at a world's fair or an honorable mention in a regional contest, she was usually inundated with letters inquiring about her pattern.

This demand was expertly tapped by the magazines, which had printed patterns from the beginning of the century, having begun chiefly as reader contributions and growing into sophisticated features where a quilt was photographed, sometimes even in a room setting, and its pattern offered at a very low cost, such as twenty-five cents. The major reason for the women's magazines' interest in patterns was not profit but service, a concept pioneered by the influential *Ladies' Home Journal*. In the twentieth century, magazines were a helping hand to women, counseling on matters of the heart, on the dust mop, and on decorating the home—all with equal aplomb. Should readers be curious about quilting, the magazines' helping hands were right there, inspiring them with cheerleading slogans: quilting was easy, fun, and anyone could make the patterns shown.

For the women's magazines, providing information about quilting was a venerable tradition, dating back to *Godey's Lady's Book* of the mid-1800s, but for the newspapers it was a significant innovation. In the late 1920s, in response to reader demand, newspapers would run Saturday or Sunday quilt columns with patterns. Often the needlework editor responsible had no quilting experience or even an interest in patchwork, but it was her job to crank out patterns on a weekly basis. In the beginning, some of these editors did considerable research in their local regions, turning up material from many grandmothers' trunks. But as the demand for patterns grew, they very often turned to the syndicated pattern companies for their column material.[48]

With names like Aunt Martha and Nancy Page, these companies seemed to have generated most of their material with staff artists, a practice that resulted in the occasional pattern that was impossible to translate from paper into fabric because of its impractical curves or angles. The large volume of designs produced is exemplified by the 800 Nancy Cabot patterns that were published in the *Chicago Tribune* in a ten-year period.[49]

The most influential of the syndicates, Home Arts and Old Chelsea Station Needlecraft Service, reached millions of women through their pattern lines. Bettina, Hope Winslow, and Colonial quilts were offered by the former, and Laura Wheeler and Alice Brooks were operated by the latter. The reason for such quaint, Betty Crocker–type names was reader appeal. Sending money to a grandmotherly woman seemed so much more personal and more like the old-fashioned, neighborly pattern exchange of an earlier era.

Of course, there were some syndicates with real people behind them, such as McKim Studios, run by artist Ruby McKim, whose book *101 Patchwork Designs* is still being published.

Perhaps the most influential sources of patterns were the batting companies: Lockport, Rock River Cotton Co., and the giant of the field, Stearns & Foster. By the late 1920s, free patterns were offered inside, and sometimes printed on, their batting covers. Stearns & Foster's Mountain Mist brand also included a number of color drawings of quilt blocks on its wrapper, probably designed by staff member Phoebe Edwards, and quilters could mail away for these for a dime. Later, Mountain Mist offered catalogues of pattern designs and sponsored extensive contests to help make the company a household word.

# PAINT BY NUMBER

In recent years, a number of quilts from the 1920s and 1930s have been referred to simply as "kit quilts." The truth is that many quilts mistakenly labeled as such were actually made from patterns. Kit sales never came close to approaching those of pattern sales, but many of the major pattern entrepreneurs did offer kits, including Marie Webster and Anne Orr. In 1922 the Ladies Art Company sold a kit with a stamped quilt top and appliqué patches for a bolster at a cost of about $5. Presewn quilt blocks could be ordered for thirty-five cents to $1.50 each (cheaper by the dozen) and completed quilts, which could be made from any design illustrated, ranged from $25.00 to $45.00, with an extra $2.00 for a scalloped edge.[50]

Kits became more popular as their packaging improved. The earliest ones were not significant time-savers. Although they did spare the quilter the necessity of buying and choosing her fabric, their designs had to be stamped by hand, a process that involved perforating a paper pattern with a tracing wheel and rubbing stamping powder, which usually came in yellow or blue, through its holes. With the advent of iron-on transfers and prestamped fabrics, kits became more lucrative. The Rainbow Quilt Company, a leader in the kit field, even stamped its designs in the colors prescribed for the appliqué or embroidery.

That kits were popular is shown by the fact that they were offered for sale by such magazines as *Good Housekeeping*, often under the magazine's own name. *Modern Priscilla* even used kits as subscription incentives. Yet even then, kits were considered controversial, something that patterns never were. Women who considered quilting an art had serious doubts about the kit trend.

Carrie Hall, writing in 1935, found the kits popularized by "this hurrying age" to be "especially distressing for the 'true quilter.'" She went on to note that there was a great comfort in the choosing of fabrics and planning of designs for quiltmaking. "How could the modern quiltmaker know that joy," she asked, "if she must go to the store and . . . buy a ready-cut quilt."[51]

Despite this lament, kits, like patterns, did have their

16, 17, 18. Quilt kit: "Early American" pattern, Paragon Needlecraft. Ca. 1935. 91" x 75". Although the majority of twentieth-century commercially offered quilt motifs were made from company patterns, kits were also available that contained most of the makings for a quilt. The box illustrated here contained a 90" x 104" percale sheet stamped to show where the maker was expected to appliqué the enclosed "color fast" cutouts and to embroider finishing details. The company recommended using "Peri-Lusta" embroidery thread. In fact, little was left to the quilter's imagination. While the more creative needleworker probably would have found this tightly controlled project somewhat inhibiting, the inexperienced or less adventurous quiltmakers benefited from this carefully structured, foolproof method of quiltmaking. (Collection of Annette and George Amann)

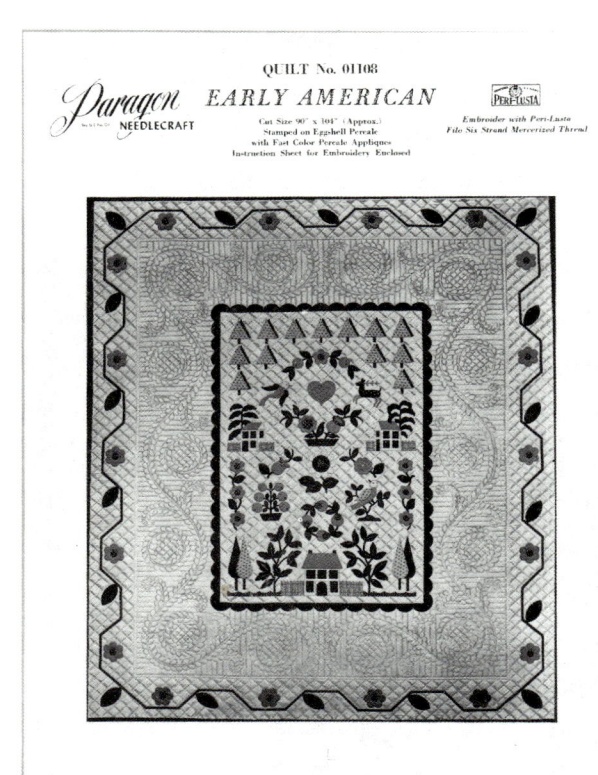

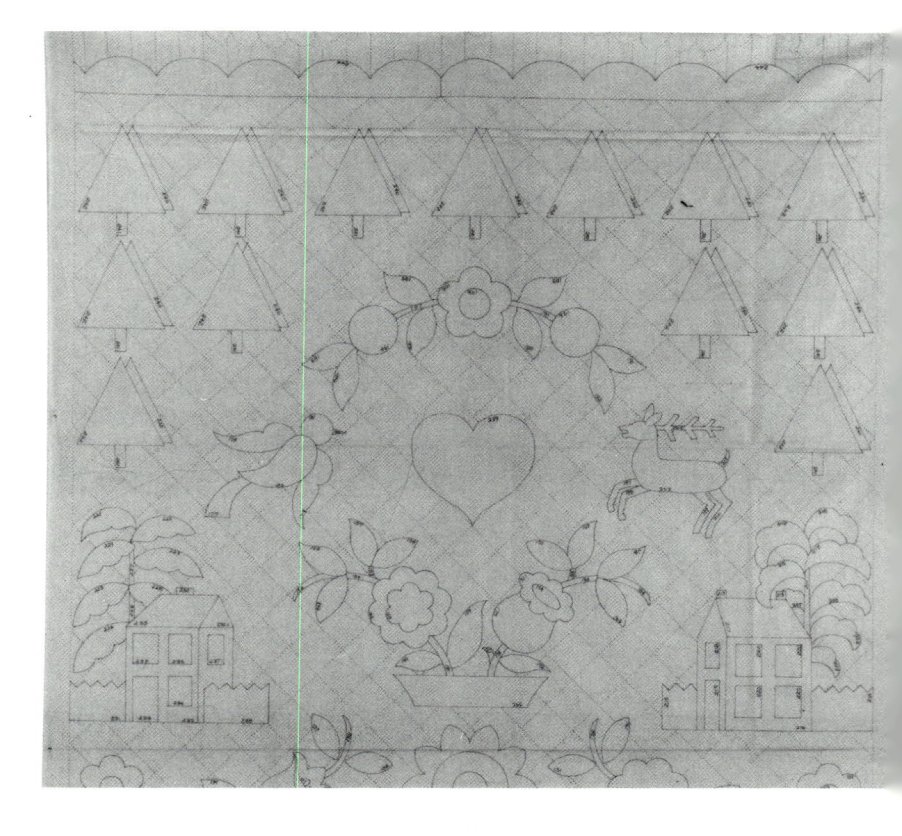

usefulness in helping quilters learn their art. Emma Andres, who went on to win a merit award at the Chicago Century of Progress contest in 1933, made her first quilt in 1931. It was an appliqué "Tiger Lily" kit, ordered from an advertisement in the January 1931 issue of *Woman's World*.

Not solely a phenomenon of the twenties and thirties, kits are still being made today by companies such as Lee Wards, Herrschners, Paragon, Bucilla, and Gold Art. Bonnie Leman's *Quilter's Newsletter Magazine* sells kits of some of their original designs, and the Smithsonian Institution, The Metropolitan Museum of Art, and the Museum of American Folk Art in New York City have offered kits, usually copies of quilts in their collections. Certain sources have even miniaturized highly acclaimed quilts and sold kits of them to be made into small wall hangings.

# AND THE WINNER IS...

The twentieth century was a time when no fair, be it county, state, or world, was complete without a quilt contest. The recognition they offered inspired many women to buy the finest fabrics and stitch the most complicated patterns in hopes of winning a blue ribbon, which, in many cases, would then be talked about and remembered for years.

"Never will I forget when the 'Le Moyne Star' that I pieced when I was seven years old took first place," wrote Carrie Hall of an 1881 county fair.[52] "Life has brought me no honor to equal that one." Often, winning a blue ribbon was the encouragement a quilter needed to pursue her talent. Mrs. Scioto Danner recalled that "her knees shook," and she almost couldn't go over to see the quilt corner after the judging at the 1930 State Fair in Topeka, Kansas. If her blocks could win ribbons and thus offer proof of her talent, she was thinking of going into the quilt-pattern business. If not, her idea "was another Depression failure." Mrs. Danner need not have worried; all her entries won either a red or blue ribbon, and a successful business was launched.

Competitions were a favorite of the magazines because they were sure to lure readers and boost circulation. Among the first was *Pictorial Review*'s National Quilting Bee Contest in 1911, which awarded first prize to Mrs. J. B. Pearce of Illinois for her "Rock Mountain" quilt. In 1922, *Comfort Magazine* in Augusta, Maine, sponsored a quilt-block contest in which the majority of entries were done in appliqué, reflecting its popularity in the twenties and the attitude held by some that appliqué was superior to piecework. A book of winners was published, but their patterns were not offered. In 1929, *Farm and Fireside* ran a similar contest and published the winning blocks in its September issue. The top prize went to a seventy-three-year-old man, G. B. Keefer of Butler, Ohio, whose pieced quilt, "The Golden Star," was judged the favorite among some 1,000 entries. It and the other winners, including the perennial "The Potted Tulip," which tied for third place, were offered as patterns. To order them, readers sent fifteen cents to the magazine.

In the flurry of contests held across the nation, it was rare for a company or manufacturer involved in quilting to overlook the promotional possibilities in sponsoring these events. Stearns & Foster held numerous contests for its Mountain Mist batting and offered patterns for the winners in its popular booklets. Pattern syndicates such as Aunt Martha offered prizes for quilt blocks as a way of gathering new patterns. Macy's and other major department stores ran quilt contests. The Eastern States Exposition held the first national quilt contest in 1932 at the restored New England village of Storrowton, part of Springfield, Massachusetts,[53] attracting 600 entries for a $50.00 first prize. In 1933 and 1936 the contest was repeated.

The granddaddy of all quilt events in the first half of the twentieth century was undoubtedly the Century of Progress competition, sponsored by Sears, Roebuck in conjunction with Chicago's 1933 Exposition. The 25,000 entries received in response to an announcement in Sears's January catalogue was quite a contrast to the last major fair previously held in Chicago. The World's Columbian Exposition of 1893 featured an important Woman's Building, but the book documenting it, *Art and Handiwork*, lists such items as elegant Belgian lace and ignores quilts. Even though they were exhibited, apparently quilts were not considered worth mentioning.

In 1933, however, the Chicago fair attracted so much attention that one newspaper of the day calculated that it inspired 25,000 people to work 5,625,000 hours on the quilts entered. Considering that the average quilt took 225 hours or twenty-eight eight-hour days to sew, it was further computed that the quilting time equaled

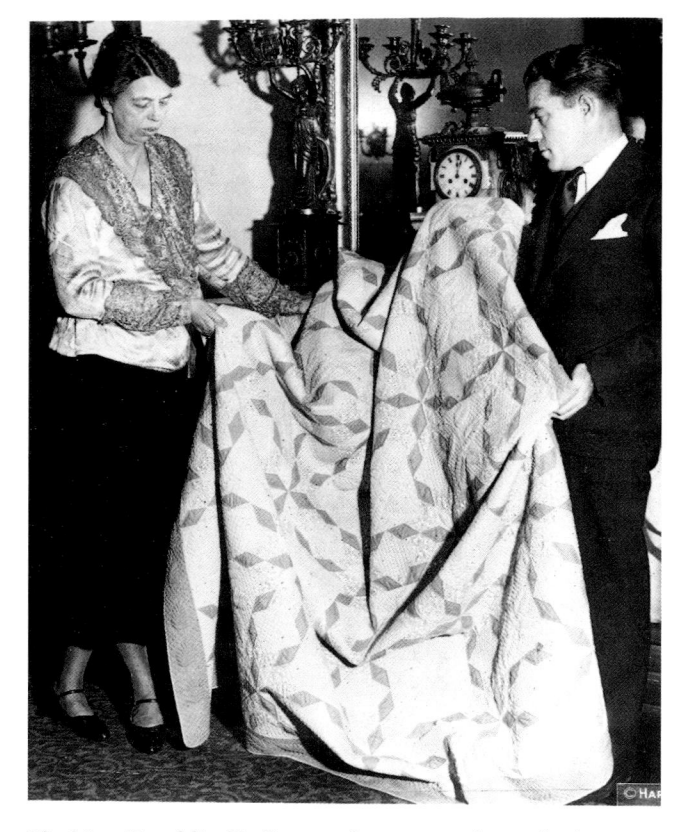

19. Mrs. Franklin D. Roosevelt accepts the quilt that won first prize in the Century of Progress in Quiltmaking Contest sponsored by Sears, Roebuck in 1933. Despite the hard times of the Great Depression, nearly 25,000 quilters found the wherewithal to complete and submit their quilts, with the top prize of $1,200 and the honor of having one's work displayed at Chicago's Century of Progress Exposition spurring them on. Photograph courtesy Sears, Roebuck and Co.

234,875 working days or 642 years.[54] Imagine putting in all that time—and winning! Texan Lois Hobgood, who had never quilted before she heard of the Sears contest, still has her two prize ribbons pinned to the "Vase of Flowers" appliqué quilt that she designed and stitched for the occasion. She won a local prize and a third place in the Dallas regional contest and had her quilt sent on to Chicago to be seen by 5,000,000 people.[55]

Part of the incentive for entering the Century of Progress competition was the hefty $1,000 First Prize and the honor of having the winning quilt given to First Lady Eleanor Roosevelt.

Thirty regional contests were held in department stores to narrow the choices for the quilts that would then be sent on to the national competition. The judges for the finals included Anne Orr, Art-Needlework Editor of *Good Housekeeping*, and other experts, including a Sears Home Advisor, a representative from the Art Institute of Chicago, and Mary A. McElwain, a quilt collector, designer, and shop owner.

Interestingly, the winning quilts fueled a great number of patterns, kits, and booklets, such as the one by Sears called *Century of Progress in Quilting* (1934), which still serves as an inspiration to contemporary quilters. The Grand Prize–winning "Eight-Point Combination Feathered Star," made by Margaret Rogers Caden of Lexington, Kentucky, was offered as a pattern in the Aunt Martha pamphlet *The Quilt Fair Comes to You*. In 1934, *Capper's Weekly* ran the pattern with this poetic caption:

> Twinkle twinkle quilted star
> Now I wonder how you are
> Pieced and padded oh so high
> For the White House bye and bye.[56]

Although the verse may leave much to be desired, the thoughts are timely. After the Margaret Caden quilt was delivered to the White House, it disappeared, and quilt historians are still wondering when and where it might reappear.[57]

A $500 second-prize winner from the Century of Progress, Mable Langley's "Colonial Rose" appliquéd spread, was offered as a kit in 1935 by The Needlecraft Supply Company of Chicago, which also produced a kit for a Kansas City regional prize winner, "Autumn Leaf." This pattern, also called "1000 Leaves" and "Running Vine Medallion" (fig. 23), was popularized even further when Charlotte Jane Whitehill made an example in 1934, which is now in The Denver Art Museum.

Among the quilts attracting attention at the fair were those exhibited by Bertha Meckstroth of Glencoe, Illinois, who was related to the Sears family. A prolific quiltmaker who liked religious themes, she gave forty-six quilts away to relatives during her lifetime. The remaining seventy-one were divided between Radcliffe College and Barat College, the result of a lawsuit after her death.

The 1939–1940 New York World's Fair sponsored "America Through the Needle's Eye," a contest that included quilting along with crochet and other needlework. It was sponsored by department stores throughout the East and West that ran preliminary contests and supplied over $3,000 in prize money. Quilters had a chance to win the $500 first prize with either old or new work (new work being a quilt completed after the contest's announcement). The winner of the old-work category, who also garnered an additional $125 by tying for the Popular Prize, was Bertha Stenge of Chicago.[58]

When Mrs. Stenge followed that national success with a $1,000 Grand Award for her "Victory" quilt in *Woman's Day*'s 1942 contest, she became somewhat of a celebrity. Women wrote to her from all over the country asking for her patterns. The magazine sent her to New York for the awards ceremony, which was broadcast over NBC radio. *Woman's Day* published Mrs. Stenge's spread in March 1943, with a caption advising readers that re-creating the quilt in cotton, complete with an appliquéd eagle, shield, and state stars, would probably cost about $6.00.[59]

The *Woman's Day* contests in the early years of World War II are among the best remembered by quilters today, partly because of the scope of their promotion. They also held a special wartime role. To enter the national contest, entrants first had to have won at the state or county level. A number of states, including Arkansas and California, canceled their state fairs during the war, so *Woman's Day* arranged special quilt contests for them.[60]

But the quilt contest is far from being a thing of the past. Many contests continue to be held in the U.S., and one of the most significant was The Great American Quilt Contest sponsored by the Scotchgard® Brand Products Group of 3M, which was a Museum of American Folk Art event presented in New York City in celebration of the Statue of Liberty Centennial, April 24–27, 1986. The Grand Prize winner of this event was Moneca Calvert of Carmichael, California, who won $20,000 for her quilt titled "Glorious Lady Freedom."

# THE PROS

The professional quiltmaker has always been a part of quilting history—the woman with exceptionally fine needlework skills whose services could be obtained for a fee. One of the most important of these is now thought to be Mary Evans of Baltimore, Maryland, who, working with a group of Methodist Church ladies in the 1840s and 1850s, produced some of the finest, most beautiful appliquéd spreads in history, the "Baltimore Album" quilts.

The twentieth-century quilter who could finish another woman's pieced or appliquéd top with fine stitchery was a woman of talent, sought out by her neighbors because of her superior skills. Often her clients came to her through personal referrals rather than because of her business savvy. Being proud of the fact that others were willing to hire her hands was often her reason for becoming a professional quilter. A relative of ours in Iowa, Great-aunt Cora, was much talked about in the family because people from all over the state sent her their spreads to be quilted. Her particular pride was the fact that her fine needlework showed through on the back of the quilt, thus making it equally beautiful on both sides.

The fees the quilters earned were literally pin money, a small supplement to the farm or family income that gave them a sense of independence. As Marie Webster noted: "Quilting is usually paid for by the amount of thread used, no consideration being given to the amount of time expended on the work. A spool of cotton thread, such as is found in every dry-goods store, averaging two hundred yards to the spool, is the universal measure."[61] She added that, in 1915, $1.00 per spool was the average price charged for such needlework, but that some quilters in more urban areas were charging $5.00 a spool.

Although most women did their own needlework or quilted with friends at a bee, hiring a professional quilter was not thought of as diminishing the artistry of the spread. A number of near-legendary makers, including Rose Kretsinger, Charlotte Jane Whitehill, and Hannah Haynes Headlee, had their quilts professionally finished. It is believed that one prominent designer even won a prize in a *Woman's Day* contest for the quilting—*not* the design—of a spread that she had sent out to a professional. The best-known quilt artists always had a firm hand in the design of the stitchery pattern and carefully supervised the needlework so that it enhanced the spread as a whole, thereby maintaining an important role in the total creative process. Occasionally, Mrs. Kretsinger did give credit to a Mrs. Brennan of Maple Hill, Kansas, for some of the quilting in her spreads.

In addition to quilting, the basting of tops was often done by professionals. In fact, since 1898, the Ladies Art Company sold presewn quilt blocks in any of its 420 patterns. Marie Webster also offered her appliqué designs as basted tops, for a more substantial fee, of course. Lillian Walker, who ran quite a successful business selling quilts, had ten women basting for her. And Nashville's Anne Orr had a retinue of quilters off in the hills of Kentucky who made spreads to her designs. Also in Kentucky, Eleanor Beard headed a cottage industry for quiltmaking, advertisements for which can be seen in issues of *The House Beautiful* from the 1920s.

Monogrammed sateen spreads even found a market, priced in 1922 at $150.00 for a double. Sisters Rosalie and Ona of the Wilkinson Art Quilts of Ligonier, Indiana, knew their market and promised to provide buyers with "prestigious, impressive works of art" by personally supervising their design and construction.

In the period under discussion, there was a boom market for handmade quilts as well as for patterns, and a woman with sewing talent could easily find extra work for her nimble fingers. Many of the professional quilters had a waiting list of at least a year. Their counterparts in the 1980s are difficult to find and their waiting lists are often discouragingly long.

One professional needleworker, Minnie Unruh of Goessel, Kansas, even found she could specialize in just marking quilts rather than sewing them. She drew the elaborate quilting designs that were then popular on plain or whole-cloth quilts in Mennonite areas, and she could finish 150 in a year. Her fees were based on the type of design to be marked, plus an additional charge for a queen- or king-size top, for which, incidentally, she recommended ample measurements: 108 by 120 inches for a queen size, and 120 by 124 inches for a king size.[62]

# AND IN THIS CORNER...

Although appliqué quilts were more popular in the 1920s and piecework was favored in the 1930s, among quiltmakers in some circles the appliqué method was considered to have socially superior overtones. The origins of this attitude are uncertain, but may be related to the fact that appliqué, as done by "aristocratic" Southern ladies, usually required buying substantial yardage in order to have enough fabric of the right color to complete an elaborate appliqué design. On the other hand, piecework could be effectively made with fabric scraps, a fact that may account for its increased popularity during the Depression.

In 1915, Marie Webster quoted a Kentucky author, Miss Bessie Daingerfield, who wrote: "To every mountain woman her piece [sic] quilts are her daily interest, but her patch [a period word for appliqué] quilts are her glory...The piece quilt is, of course, made of scraps, and its beauty or ugliness depends on the colors that come to hand, the intricacy of the design, and one's skill in executing it . . . a patch quilt...is made for the generations that come after."[63]

Carrie Hall, writing twenty years later, reported that appliqué or "laid-on" quilts were considered more elegant than their humble pieced cousins. She felt that an "appliquéd quilt is apt to be a more artistic expression of the quilter's craft, in that it is created 'out of whole cloth,' so to speak, and offers correspondingly greater freedom for the expression of the designer's artistic capabilities."[64] She added, however, that "the pieced quilt, though considered in the old days as inferior...is today almost equally valued because of the excellence of some of the designs, and because of its association with the four-poster bed of olden times."[65]

Ruth Finley refers to the function of quilts as a decorative element in the household, with the best quilts saved for "dressing up" for socially important visitors. The best spreads reserved for such events were invariably appliqué. With this practice, the appliqué quilt became a "kind of social barometer," indicating the importance, or lack thereof, of one's callers.[66]

Detractors of piecework apparently have never been much impressed by examples of quite spectacular artistry in piecework. Several quilters of this period truly outdid themselves by creating spreads composed of innumerable pieces. Such quilts were often quite stupefying and perhaps not always as dazzling in their overall beauty as in their construction; yet the

20. General store, Birney, Montana. June 1939. A dry-goods counter, complete with quilting supplies, athletic shorts, shirts, and American flags would be enticing to anyone. However, this kitten has clearly mistaken the straw hats for the feline exercise department. Photograph by Arthur Rothstein. (Library of Congress)

21 (above). Cotton prints. 1900–1915. Unlike the bright pastel prints of the 1920s, these fabrics of the earliest years of the twentieth century reflect the transition from the darker palette of the Victorian era with traditional tiny motifs. Fabrics courtesy Carter Houck.

22 (below). Cotton prints. 1930–1940. After World War I, with resumed access to German dyes and refinements in the American textile industry, fabrics blossomed with cheery prints and colors that quilters craved. Fabrics courtesy Carter Houck.

23. Detail of vine appliqué. The fabric petals stitched to the vines of this commercial pattern provide us with a good survey of cotton prints popular in the late 1930s and early 1940s.

quiltmakers attained a niche in quilt history. When the statement is made that quilters of the second quarter of the twentieth century enjoyed piecework with unbridled enthusiasm, one may even go a step further and suggest that a few of the devotees were on the brink of going to pieces.

Extraordinary pride and patience are evidenced by a pieced quilt of pioneer times cited by Carrie Hall[67] as containing 30,000 pieces, each measuring 1¼ by ¾ inches. She remarked that it would be difficult for a twentieth-century woman "in these days of hurry and stress" to find the time or the inclination to undertake such a mammoth project. The unprecedented "hurry and stress" of the 1980s make the 1920s examples of "E Pluribus Unum" seem almost prehistoric.

There appears to have been a rivalry between the sexes as to who could piece a quilt with the most patches. When the St. Louis *Post-Dispatch* reported that a quilt made with 21,840 patches established a new world's record, a quilter named Jane Long resolved to take action. In five months in her seventy-eighth year, she retaliated with a quilt made with 38,000 patches.[68] In rebuttal to this achievement, Albert Small of Ottawa, Illinois, using dime-size hexagons, assembled a monumental mosaic of 63,460 pieces. A journal kept by Emma Andres in 1944 logs one of her piecework projects, a copy of Charles Pratt's "Ninety and Nine." Her entries were understandably brief: "Feb. 3—2,685 pieces. Feb. 13—3,365 pieces. July 19—added 38 pieces. July 20—75 pieces added...."[69]

It is interesting to note that following World War II, British quilters were severely limited by the rationing of clothing and materials, which necessitated recycling every possible scrap of material. The many-pieced "Honeycomb" pattern, long popular in England, was particularly adaptable to the use of precious bits of hoarded fabric. By this time, America's extremely popular "Grandmother's Flower Garden," a cousin of England's "Honeycomb" and earlier "Mosaic" designs, was firmly established in homes across America.

# KITSCH AS KITSCH CAN

As in clothing, fads in quilting have come and gone over the years. The "Crazy" quilt was certainly a grand passion for a while. Was there any quilter in the late nineteenth century who did not make at least one? With such intense interest in quilting in the twenties and thirties, it is not surprising that a number of eccentric quilts would be made. One pleasing example of a style in which it was easy to get carried away with a gimmick is the "Yo-yo" quilt (fig. 198). It was fashioned with circles of fabric, the edges of which were gathered in toward the center to resemble a soda-bottle cap with the sides flattened inward. The center opening of the circles was sometimes filled with a bright bit of contrasting fabric to give this unique mosaic even more dazzle.[70]

Another design quirk was the "Puff," which looked like golf-ball-size wads of fabric sewn together. When folded, this spread could require a full closet of its own because of its bulk, and some examples of this style are far better left in the closet. "Puff" quilts were also called "Biscuit" and "Bun," for obvious reasons.

Quilts made from slinky lingerie fabrics also appeared on the scene, as if Jean Harlow had done some quilting between takes on the movie set. One quilt we have seen that truly stretched the point was made from corset fabric, thus giving new shape and form to the ever-expanding concept of quilting.

As if to take up some of the slack(s) in their quilting creativity, a number of needleworkers made alterations in their work schedules to include the fashioning of a "pants quilt." In a style tailor-made to their tastes, this item was not a quilt with legs but rather a spread made from "father's discarded breeches."[71]

Quilts have been adorned with buttons, sequins, ostrich feathers, photographs (requiring the use of chemicals), cellophane, jewelry, hardware, and endless accessories. Quilts have also been shaped into other forms, crossing the border between quilting and soft sculpture, and between good taste and bad. A recent foray into the world of the-latest-thing artistry, employing quilting materials and techniques, resulted in the creation of a giant fabric reproduction of a roll of bathroom tissue.

In more traditional quilts, quality varies even in the name of the patterns. While some of the more memorable names such as "Delectable Mountains" or "Philadelphia Pavement" ring rather nicely, there are a number of pattern names described by Marie Webster as "grotesque."[72] Among the more amusing names were "Hairpin Catcher," which featured actual pockets

24. "A Meeting of the Sunbonnet Children." 1978. 100″ x 104″. Made by Betty Hagerman, Sweepstakes Winner at the Kansas State Fair, 1978. What if all the Sunbonnet Sues and Sunbonnnet Sams of quilting history were gathered together on one spread? That's the question this contemporary quilter answered with her mind-boggling, one-stop shopping list of the various shapes that these charming but faceless children have taken. Here is a remarkable, succinct summary of most of the sweet figures that kept popping up in twentieth-century quilts. Photograph courtesy *Quilter's Newsletter Magazine*.

for overnight storage of hairpins, "Tangled Garters," and "The X quisite." One of the strangest names is "Hearts and Gizzards," although the pattern itself is a particularly pleasing one and deserving of a more agreeable cognomen.

One novel quilt in a more traditional style was made of 33,782 half-inch triangles of silk grosgrain ribbon, a project that Sarah A. Haynes of Gladwin, Michigan, began in 1892 and completed seventeen years later. The reward for her labor was a $15 first prize at the 1929 Women's International Exposition in Detroit. More unusual than the familiar silk cigar-band quilts of the late 1800s, her triangles were joined on the reverse side, thereby forming an overall honeycomb pattern.

Another unique method of construction involved sewing little triangles and then assembling them in an overlapping arrangement similar to that used in a type of rugmaking.

The "Charm" quilt was also a technical tour de force. A style with its roots in the late 1800s, its claim to fame was that it had no two fabrics alike. The pieced blocks were sewn together with no dividing sashing. Surviving examples are often pieced triangle or pyramid patterns, offering a mean challenge to contemporary quilt lovers who attempt to find repeated calicoes in the spread. In August 1923, *Hearth and Home* printed instructions for a "Charm" quilt. Numerous variations appeared elsewhere under new names such as "Joseph's Coat, K1026" in *Everyday Life* in July 1930. That publication's columnist went a bit far in arbitrarily borrowing another well-known pattern's name. She suggested what amounted to a further dilution of the pattern by using only twenty-five different fabric designs with a few plain colors mixed in to achieve what she thought was the same effect.

Continuing in the tradition of the delightful "Lady's Boot" (fig. 65), made in Kentucky in the 1890s, common objects were often cut from fabric and appliquéd on quilts in the twentieth century. Among the era's quilt writers, some, such as Ruth Finley, felt such examples as "The Old Town Pump" and "Horse Shoe" were "hopeless entirely."[73] Her point is well taken, especially in light of the Ladies Art Company pattern that featured a mouse as the single repeated motif. More appealing cutout-motif quilts such as "Schoolhouse" (fig. 109) and "Umbrella" (fig. 68) enjoyed great popularity and now, as precursors of Pop Art images of the recent past, are especially sought by collectors.

One popular design that has been subjected to some contemporary abuse is the ubiquitous "Sunbonnet Sue" (fig. 24). Her familiar silhouette with its large bonnet hiding her head is found with such frequency that a friend of ours quipped, "it robs one of the will to live." "Sunbonnet Sue" however, has a very interesting past,

25. Thrifty Egg Mash bags. February 1939. Chicken feed, flour, and bulky products were bagged in printed cotton materials suitable for dresses, with valued leftovers saved for patchwork. Photograph by Russell Lee. (Library of Congress)

dating back to British illustrator Kate Greenaway. In the 1870s her figures with rapt, bonnet-shrouded faces, making them seem absorbed in a private world, became popular on greeting cards and illustrated countless books. In the United States, a later, more direct source for "Sunbonnet Sue" is *The Sunbonnet Babies Primer*, illustrated by Bertha L. Corbett and published by Rand, McNally in 1902. From that point until the 1930s, 1,300,000 first graders learned to read from these primers adorned with amply bonneted little girls. One of the earliest versions of these figures as quilt patterns is "Sunbeam Babies," an embroidered series by Frank's Art Needlework, St. Louis, published in 1905. Later, Marie Webster offered "Sunbonnet Lassies," eight elaborate figures by a picket fence with quilted sunflowers. The interpretations continued endlessly, and patterns were offered by just about every source in the business.[74]

Another design novelty was that of using state motifs like "Arkansas Star," "Texas Tulip," and "North Carolina Lily," some of which were based on very old patterns. A 1930s Nancy Cabot clipping, which claimed "every state in the union has contributed to the quilt album with a rose pattern bearing its name," set quilt historian Cuesta Benberry of St. Louis, Missouri, and her fellow pattern collectors searching for the forty-eight roses that could have been part of the quilting union at that time. Although they found more than forty-eight patterns, some states had no roses,

26. Detail from an embroidered flour-sack quilt. Dated 1933. Cloth flour sacks were routinely recycled by frugal housewives as dishtowels and as fabric for quilt backs. Here one quilter, enamored with the sack motifs, collected twenty-five different bags for the squares of her quilt, an effort that may have involved the help of distant relatives. (Collection of Joanna S. Rose)

while others like Kentucky and Ohio had more than their share of local rose variations. One "Ohio Rose" shared by Ruth Snyder came as a premium from a radio station in the early days of broadcasting.[75]

Another type of quilt to be found in this period was the feed-sack quilt. In the days before paper and plastic packaging, farm-animal feed came in big cloth sacks. Open up the seams and you had a good-size piece of fabric. Although of a common-grade cotton, many of the sacks were decorated with floral prints (fig. 25). The print a farmer bought was of concern to his wife and daughters because their quilts, not to mention their dresses, were quite often made from the feed-sack fabric. So buying feed was a big event. Sometimes people would stand outside the store and trade fabrics so that instead of having two yards each of two prints, you could acquire four yards of one.[76]

Sugar and flour also came in sacks that were recruited as fabric for dish towels, tablecloths, and quilts. Although feed sacks were frequently used for the front of a quilt, these smaller sacks were usually relegated to the back. Manufacturers seemed to realize that their packaging would be recycled, as their logos usually could be bleached out. A notable exception to most quilters' desire to disguise the fact that they were using feed sacks is the "O.K. Flour" sack quilt (fig. 26).

The diminutive size of a tobacco pouch didn't faze Pearl Thate of Carrollton, Missouri. When she was a girl around 1918, she and her siblings used to sell garden vegetables to two boardinghouses in town. On the way back to their farm Pearl would look for discarded tobacco pouches, which measured only 3 by 4 inches. Determined to make a quilt, she removed their strings, opened their sides, and finally acquired enough fabric to piece her first spread![77]

# NOT FOR WOMEN ONLY

Since the invention of the loom in 2640 B.C. by a Chinese woman, Lady of Si-ling, whose husband was Emperor Huang-ti,[78] textiles and needlework traditionally have been the province of women. History records several significant breaks in that tradition, however, including the number of twentieth-century men who turned to quilting for the same reasons that intrigued their better halves—personal expression, solace, and a fascination with the art.

Albert Small, for example, born in High Wycombe, England, in 1885, came to America and worked as a foreman in a sand company, handling heavy machinery and explosives. After a hard day's work, he found relaxation in quilting "...in spare moments after dinner at night...I start with a star and make it up as I go along."[79] His quilt, containing a staggering 63,000 patches, is certainly evidence of his determination with a needle.

In her book *Historic Quilts*, Florence Peto mentions a doctor who quilted between his chores at a busy New York City hospital.[80] He had been a naval officer during World War I and learned to sew as an enlisted man. After the war, he was inspired to take up quilting after visiting a quilt exhibition at Wanamaker's department store in Philadelphia. For his first project he chose a cube-work or "Tea Boxes" pattern, which required careful engineering of light and dark diamond-shaped patches, using silks from neckties and samples given to him by a nurse. It took 650 patches, 290 feet of stitching, and approximately seven months to complete this particular operation.

Mrs. Peto also referred to Harry D. Kendig of

Windber, Pennsylvania, who preferred commercial patterns for his quilt designs but always chose the color schemes himself. Taught expert needlework techniques by his mother, who wanted to keep him busy after school, he found quilting in his later years a relaxing contrast to the rigors of his varied work as a carpenter, bricklayer, railroad repairman, and carshop foreman. Asked why he liked to make quilts, he replied, as many a woman might have, "First, I might say it takes my mind off my daily work, and next, well, I make them because I like to."[81] In 1932, Kendig proudly stated, "No other needle but mine goes into the making...if anyone else took a stitch in my quilt, I'd take it out." Obviously, the social quilting bee held little appeal for him.

Joseph P. Deibert of Schnecksville, Pennsylvania, was inspired to make his quilt, "God's Autumn Cover," in the fall of 1934 "when nature was robed in her most beautiful colors." While visiting his cousin in Allentown, Pennsylvania, he commented that it would take a "Master Artist" to paint a picture as dazzling as the one nature had created. His cousin suggested that the picturesque scene would make a wonderful quilt. Deibert then gathered thirty-six leaves and reproduced their exact shape and size in a rainbow of appliqués. He enlisted his housekeeper, Mrs. Emma Reichard, to make the quilt. It was completed after about four months over the winter of 1934/35.

E. R. Dickerson, a retired life-insurance executive, took up quilting to replace a growing habit of snoozing after dinner in his easy chair. He re-created his "Louisville Male High School" from a pen-and-ink sketch by his son Norvin, a 1910 graduate of the school. Mr. Dickerson was concerned with the architectural motifs and the accuracy of details. He presented the quilt to his son for his birthday.

Charles Easterly, a Pennsylvania farmer, made over thirty quilts at his home near Allentown. He quilted for pleasure and refused to accept money to copy one of his quilts, preferring instead to give them away and enjoy his "art for art's sake."[82] One of his quilts, done entirely by hand, contains more than 9,000 triangular patches.

Charles Pratt, an immigrant from Manchester, England, traveled across this country exhibiting his prize quilts, which were shown in 1911 at the Montgomery County Fair near Philadelphia. Pratt created extraordinary mosaic picture quilts with tiny silk squares. As these were not backed or quilted, they were not quilts in the traditional sense, but rather pieced spreads. His admirable "Ninety and Nine" depicts the Good Shepherd holding the strayed lamb. "Penn's Treaty," also made in small squares, was in the silhouette style. Florence Peto exhibited his quilts, especially "Ninety and Nine," at many of her lectures and maintained an active correspondence with him. On his death in 1942 at the age of eighty-nine, his daughter gave "Ninety and Nine" to Mrs. Peto. Of the men who quilted, Charles Pratt, who won almost 450 prize ribbons, acquired a significant reputation and a following in what was then a woman's world.

# FLIGHTS OF FANCY

The twentieth-century needlework revival was not limited to quiltmaking, conventional or otherwise. Embroidery, crocheting, needlepoint, and even stenciling and painting on fabric all gained in popularity, and embroidery in particular found its way into quilting.

Embroidery in the first decades of the 1900s bore little resemblance to the "workt" spreads of eighteenth- and early nineteenth-century America, although floral and urn motifs remained particularly suited to the art. The sometimes rather heavy-branded black embroidery often used to outline the whimsical appliquéd butterflies and "Dresden Plates" of the 1920s and 1930s could be a twentieth-century reincarnation of the black-silk outline stitchery on linen called "blackwork" or "Spanish work," which dates from quilts of sixteenth-century England. According to tradition, the Spanish wife of Henry VIII, Catherine of Aragon, introduced this popular needlework style into England, although it probably originated in ancient Persia and China.[83]

"Etching on linen," or outline embroidery, was popular with quiltmakers in the late 1800s and early 1900s, but was most often done with turkey red thread on white muslin, using Kate Greenaway-type bonneted figures.

Cross-stitch embroidery, resembling the stitchery in nineteenth-century samplers, became particularly fashionable (fig. 57). One could make a pattern by using a graph on which the design—often a basket of flowers—was sketched and transferred to the fabric. It was then stitched with colored embroidery threads, which the Artamo Thread Co., among other suppliers, eagerly provided, along with booklets, kits, and instructions.

Printed embroidery patterns were also readily available, such as the vase-shaped basket of flowers offered in the August 1919 issue of *Modern Priscilla*. The quilt to be embellished in this way alternated embroidered 6½ by 8-inch blocks of unbleached sheeting with plain blue or pink blocks of mercerized pongee, a treated, silklike fabric. One advantage of using this pattern was that the needleworker could easily carry the small blocks to work on while visiting a friend.

"Cloth Picture Books" were suggested as a home project by *Modern Priscilla* in 1928.[84] Unbleached muslin "pages" were first colored with crayon, then pressed from the back with an iron to set the color, and finally outlined with stitching. The magazine, unfortunately, suggested machine stitching for the outlining, apparently in an effort to please busy housewives. Hand embroidery, such as that outlining the charming Kate Greenaway figures, would have been the more likely choice of selective needleworkers of the day.

Under the banner "Christmas 1929," the same publication suggested giving the needlework projects on its pages as Christmas gifts. These included a wall panel that required darning skills to complete a colorful peacock motif, which closely resembles Hannah Headlee's later "Peacock" quilt (fig. 182). Other items included doilies, pillows, quilt blocks, and a felt flower corsage to be worn on a coat.

Numerous publications contributed to the wealth of handcraft projects, including *The Country Gentleman*, *McCall's*, and *American Home Pattern Book*, which offered crochet patterns in the 1940s, as well as large companies, such as Sears, Roebuck and J.C. Penney, which copyrighted its felt pillow and chintz picture kits in 1931.

Among the patterns designed by Marie Webster in 1915 for *The Ladies' Home Journal* was an appliqué rose on fine linen that could be applied to all bedroom appointments, including cushions, chair covers, table covers, bureau and chiffonier scarves, and utility bags to create an indoor rose-garden effect. *Woman's Day*, *The Detroit Free Press*, *Comfort Magazine*, and virtually every other publication seeking women as readers urged housewives to get to work on myriad projects. These included towels and aprons to sell at church bazaars, luncheon sets with place mats and tumbler doilies for shower gifts, stuffed toys, curtains, bookends, kitchen-wall hangings with calendars attached, pot holders, a three-dimensional "breakfast cloth," baby clothes, a "Hot Iron Reminder," washer tub and wringer covers with fruit made from fade-proof Peter Pan cloth, bridge "tallies" that convert into place cards, handbags, clothespin bags, utility bags, and duster bags.

Should any free time be left over once these projects were completed, one could take on handstitched taffeta comforters, candlewick spreads, tied bedcovers, and, time and energy permitting, the creation of original quilt blocks with scissors and folded papers, such as a circle of paper dolls singing "Ring-around-the-rosie."[85]

# CHANGING TIMES

Despite the "Victory" quilts that flourished during World War II, the feverish interest in quilting was past its peak when the war years arrived. In some ways it had reached such a pinnacle of popularity that there was no direction for it to go but down. However, several very tangible factors contributed to the decline of interest in quilting at the end of the first half of the twentieth century.

First, thousands of women were recruited into the wartime labor force to work in factories and to fill men's jobs in other fields, in addition to running their homes. Obviously, their free time became minimal. Second, fabric became scarcer and more expensive.

Pattern companies also had to struggle with the rising cost of paper. Many leading figures in quiltmaking and pattern design turned to other pursuits: Ruby McKim to dolls, and Carrie Hall to fashion, for example.

When America came back from the war, it was a very different era. The modern age had become the atomic age. The women who had quilted the "Navy Wives" design suggested by *The Ladies' Home Journal* became brides themselves, and their interests turned to babies, mortgages, fin-tailed cars, television, and all the diversions that postwar prosperity had to offer. In the fifties, the shape of the times was modern—from the inexpensive plywood furniture pioneered by Charles

27. Detail from an "Ocean Waves" presentation quilt. Inscribed: "To Babe from Mama 1928." Babe must have cherished Mama's 1928 quilt, since it is certainly in mint condition, providing a good reference for dating period fabrics. The cheerful border treatment frames a colorful twentieth-century update of a nineteenth-century quilt pattern. Photograph courtesy Noreen Lewandowski.

Eames to the kidney-shape coffee tables and "prefab" suburban houses. The whole point of fifties design was not to re-create an early, antique, Colonial era but to forge ahead and shape familiar objects anew. Even fabrics became man-made. Dacron was introduced by Du Pont in 1951, about the time acrylic was unveiled. Lightweight and wrinkle-proof, it seemed as if it and the earlier nylon and rayon would supplant cotton in clothing. In any case, these synthetics were uninspiring to quilters.

What is remarkable about quilting prior to 1950 was how well it fitted into an era that was hurtling toward modernity and all its attendant changes. The quilting medium adapted equally well to the curves of Art Nouveau, the angles of Art Deco, and the totally different aesthetics of Amish and Hawaiian design. It worked perfectly with the cheery pastels of the twenties and thirties, which embodied an entirely new spirit that contrasted strongly with that symbolized by the dark maroons and rusts of the Victorian era. Furthermore, quilting suited a wide range of women, from farmers' wives to the sophisticates of the jazz age, some of whom were Dr. Dunton's "nervous ladies."

That quilting not only survived into the twentieth century but also flourished seems, on the surface, an anomaly. But the quilt revival of the twenties and thirties satisfied a very deep need in America—a need to tap into a tradition of handiwork that was vanishing from women's lives as their homes became more automated with the sewing machine, the automatic washer, the vacuum cleaner, and other high-tech trappings of modernity. Particularly during the Depression, quilting gave women a profound sense of accomplishment, of being able to *do* something at a time when the labor force was idle and to *piece* something together when many people's lives were falling apart.

With each decade since this remarkable flurry of quiltmaking activity, people seemed to believe that quiltmaking would at last be buried with many of the great folk arts of the nineteenth century. So when they consider the quilting scene today, they are astonished by its broad popularity and consider it to be still another revival. It seems far more accurate, however, to think of quilt history as being one continuous unbroken thread, with interest surging in certain decades only to diminish in others. Periods of low interest occurred in the nineteenth century particularly around the time of the Civil War, as well as around 1900 and in the 1950s and 1960s. But even in these bleak periods women quilted. And they will keep on quilting because the basic needs that quilting satisfies are a rare mix of the artistic, the spiritual, and the practical.

The high standards of quilting that were reestablished in the first half of the twentieth century provide a constant inspiration and an awesome challenge to quilters today. The originality, vigor, charm, and beauty that these quilts offer set an example of creative expression open to ordinary people, who aimed for the highest quality of workmanship and, occasionally, achieved greatness. And that is the very essence of folk expression in America.

# COLLECTING TWENTIETH CENTURY QUILTS

Collecting twentieth-century quilts can be a rewarding project for a number of reasons, not the least of which is the fact that prices are still quite reasonable, especially when compared to earlier quilts of fine quality. In contrast to other areas of folk art and decorative arts, many of the better examples—those that will increase most in value—can still be found.

Quilts of the twentieth century are just beginning to be discovered by collectors who have overlooked them, perhaps from a prejudice against the sweetness and sentimentality of some of their motifs. These quilts may simply have seemed too common, too fresh in our memories, or even too commercial. Until recently, however, some of the same comments could have been made about twentieth-century weathervanes and whirligigs, whose special qualities were not appreciated for many years.

Under the headline "Twentieth Century Soars," *The New York Times* reported fierce bidding at auctions of twentieth-century decorative arts. Some collectors today would rather buy a superlative twentieth-century object than an older piece of lesser quality. At Sotheby's (in New York City), for example, a vitrine made around 1908 in Vienna recently brought an astonishing $275,000 at auction. And at Christie's (also in New York), intense bidding on a lacquered metal vase, made around 1925 by Jean Dunand of Paris, reached $71,500. Although these objects are younger than the one hundred-year span that is traditionally used to mark a piece as antique, the prices they garnered rival those of eighteenth-century decorative objects.[86]

What makes a twentieth-century quilt superlative? One guideline, generally new to the century, is the name of the maker. Just as furniture designed by the top names of the period—Josef Hoffmann and Marcel Breuer, for example—are much sought after, so are the quilts created by such top artists as Rose Kretsinger, Grace Snyder, Lillian Walker, Dr. Jeannette Throckmorton, and Bertha Meckstroth. In other centuries, quilters such as these would most likely have remained anonymous, but in the 1900s the quilts of talented makers were beribboned at fairs and eagerly published by the magazines. Although quilts made by many of the women mentioned are in private collections and museums, the work of less-publicized yet exemplary makers can often be found and documented, whether within an Amish community or a small midwestern city.

Moreover, a number of the women who entered the most famous contests—the Chicago Century of Progress in 1933, the New York World's Fair in 1939-1940 and the *Woman's Day* contests in the early '940s—are still alive. Conversations with them are a prized experience, and one need not travel too far into rural America to find a quilter who will pass along many enlightening remembrances about quilting in the first half of the twentieth century.

Another guideline for collectors of any object is condition. As in the case of a number of nineteenth-century spreads, the finest quilts made between 1900 and 1950 often appear never to have been used. This pristine condition is very desirable and has several possible causes. Sometimes family heirlooms did not always coincide with a younger generation's decorating style. It is fortunate that these unused quilts were folded and kept safely in blanket chests rather than used as bedding for the family pet, as happened in some cases. Generally, twentieth-century quilts were constructed with sturdy, colorfast fabrics and are practical for home use. They should be handled with care to ensure preservation.

In collecting twentieth-century quilts, it is interesting to note that the double-bed size that Sears, Roebuck listed in its 1902 catalogue—54 inches in width—remains the standard today. A single bed in its catalogue measured a generous 42 inches. Beds were often listed as being six feet long, although one heavy iron bed was six and a half feet, weighing in at 150 pounds.[87] Visitors to our gallery are continually surprised by the size of quilts from the past, with some measuring over 120 inches square. But early nineteenth-century beds were often quite large, and several family members occupied them on winter nights. In addition, they were generally high up off the cold floors and provided storage space for trundle beds underneath. In the twentieth century, however, quilt sizes became standardized, their dimensions dictated by prominent batting and pattern companies like Stearns & Foster.

One of the most important considerations in collecting twentieth-century quilts is whether the piece possesses any unusual or original qualities. Highly desirable are out-of-the-ordinary imaginative quilts whose makers were unafraid to depart from tradition or to infuse their work with personal feeling and real creativity. Even quilts made from patterns may contain variations that are original, thus separating them from more ordinary examples. Recently, such a quilt was brought to our shop. It showed house, flower, and bird motifs, appearing as if the quilter had taken her favorite patterns and artfully arranged them on one quilt (fig. 111).

By closely studying twentieth-century quilts, one can begin to acquire a sixth sense about which quilts were made from patterns. If the design seems just a bit too precise or uniform, particularly when a motif is repeated, our suspicions are aroused. One charming quilt we saw recently was made with little birds sitting on birdhouses. It had an appealing, colorful naiveté, and we had never seen a design like it. However, both Cuesta Benberry and Barbara Brackman, author of the *Encyclopedia of Pieced Quilt Patterns*, confirmed our hunch that it was a commercial design (fig. 75). Why was it so rare? Some patterns were neither widely published nor widely bought, but even if they had been, there is a fairly good chance that the quilts were "used up"—worn out on the bed or through the frequent washing that the light pastel and white quilts of the twentieth century often required.

Barbara Brackman's *Encyclopedia* is a valuable resource for all collectors. Comprising eight volumes of continually updated information on the quilt patterns published since 1850, it is set out as a visual reference work. The hundreds of quilt patterns sketched on its pages are sensibly classified "by the way they look."[88] This exhaustive survey is extremely useful in identifying patterns, especially those of the early twentieth century, which have long been puzzling and often misnamed or incorrectly attributed. The author confines her listings to the earliest published source for each pattern, suggesting that those who wish to pursue a particular design further might turn to *The Quilt Pattern Index* by Linda Shogren.[89] This source contains a cross-reference for a number of patterns, should one wish to track down every mention of a particular design.

After compiling eight volumes of information, author Brackman concedes that the task of cataloguing quilt patterns is never ending, and welcomes additional information from readers. With her kind permission, a comprehensive reference list that includes many of the people and companies prominent in the first half of the twentieth century is reprinted at the end of this book.

# DISPLAYING TWENTIETH CENTURY QUILTS

When hung on the wall as art, even the most exquisite quilt can be considered a bargain. The same investment would not buy a painting of comparable quality or uniqueness and, in many cases, paintings do not appreciate in value so steadily. Therefore, if a quilt is to be hung, care should be taken to use a proper method.

One of the simplest ways of hanging a quilt is with Velcro, handsewn to the top edge of the back. The needle should catch just the backing of the quilt and should not go all the way through to the front. A second, matching strip should be stapled to a piece of molding, which can then be hung on the wall. Or the Velcro can be attached to the wall directly without the molding for support. In some cases, a staple gun can be used for this step. In addition to Velcro at the top of your quilt, you might want to hand-sew squares of Velco in each of the bottom corners and in places where the quilt buckles, in order to keep the edges smooth. Again, Velcro should be attached to the wall in corresponding places. Some people like to edge quilts entirely in Velcro for a neat, stretched border.

Grosgrain ribbon can also be used to hang a quilt to the wall. First, hand-sew a strip to the top edge of the back of the quilt, catching only the quilt backing with the needle, to form a pocket. Then slide a piece of flat molding into the pocket and attach to the wall with sawtooth picture hangers, found at framing stores.

A more ambitious method of hanging a quilt involves creating a frame that resembles a canvas stretcher, cut to the exact dimensions of the quilt. Velcro is attached to the perimeter of the frame and the quilt. Both are then hung on the wall like a very large picture. This is a particularly effective way to display a quilt, and it allows for easy removal for cleaning or storage. If hinges are built into the frame, it can be folded and handily stored.

Another hanging method popularized by New York's Graphic Arts Gallery is to hand-sew a muslin border, approximately ten inches wide, on the back edge of the quilt, stitching on the lines of the binding stitches to hide the sewing. This muslin is used as a flap, which is then stretched around a wood frame and stapled to it. With this method, no potentially damaging staples, pins, or tacks are used on the quilt.

A more permanent—and expensive—framing method is to use Plexiglas, but this should be done only by very experienced framers. A Plexiglas box with an open back for "breathing" provides an elegant, more formal finish for the quilt and protects it from dampness and air pollutants, one of the worst of which is cigarette or cigar smoke. Ultraviolet Plexiglas offers some protection from fading, although a bit of the textural charm of the quilt is lost, and an element of formality accompanies the pressed-behind-Plexiglas method. Ideally, the plastic should not touch the fabric, if possible, although this makes the frame more fragile. Again, personal preference and budgetary considerations should be one's guide for framing choices.

Although direct or even bright, indirect light can cause fading of the more fugitive dyes (dark greens and reds from Pennsylvania are among the most common casualties), a quilt can hardly be enjoyed if stored in a closet. Therefore, it is advisable to choose a pleasing location on a wall that does not get direct or reflected sunlight and to inspect the quilt regularly for signs of fading. If such signs appear, either alter the lighting, perhaps by shading or adding a sun-screening treatment to your windows, or move the quilt to a new location.

# QUILT CARE

Many quilts have been damaged or destroyed by well-meaning people obsessed with cleanliness, using harsh detergents and bleaches that considerably weaken old textiles. Try to resist the temptation to achieve the "whiter whites," of the television commercials. Dirt can damage textiles when allowed to stay in the fibers, however, so cleaning is sometimes a necessity.

Washing is the most desirable cleaning method for pieces that can be washed safely. Each fabric should be tested first. Use soap and water on a cotton swab to assess colorfastness. If running occurs—embroidery thread is one of the worst offenders—dry cleaning by a fine dry cleaner who is familiar with fragile textiles is recommended. Some yellowing on white muslins may occur, but if done carefully by an experienced specialist, the safety of dry cleaning may be worth the slight alteration of appearance caused by the residue of cleaning chemicals.

For washing, a mild soap is recommended, in some cases together with an all-color bleaching powder, which can help set the colors and whiten the white muslins. An old-fashioned product, Orvis, is suitably gentle. Very cold water is preferable. Allow the quilt to soak face down, so that when it is handled, the back takes most of the strain and the weight of the water. Gently squeeze out soapy water, rinse two or three times in clean, cold water; then, as an optional step for the final rinse, add a small amount of a gentle, unscented fabric softener to the water. This will add fluffiness to the quilt when dry and bring out the quilting patterns. Allow to dry stretched on a flat surface of towels or sheets, or, for apartment dwellers, over a shower curtain rod covered with towels, changing its position frequently to avoid creases.

Quilts should be out and enjoyed as much as possible, but there are times when they must be stored, perhaps for the rotation of a collection. They should be placed in clean cloth bags and kept in a blanket chest or closet that is dry and moderate in temperature. High heat, such as that in an attic, may cause discoloration. Naturally, severe damage from leaking water, rodents, and moths are all dangers to watch for. Plastic should never be used for long periods of storage, nor should paper, unless it is the specially prepared, high-rag-content, acid-free type used by museums. Acid-free paper and cartons may be purchased from specialty stores, such as Talas, 213 West 35th Street, New York, N.Y. 10001.

# NOTES

1. *Quilter's Journal* (Mill Valley, Calif.) 3, no. 4 (Winter 1980/81), p. 9.
2. Barbara Brackman, "Looking Back at the Great Quilt Contest," *Quilter's Newsletter Magazine* (October 1983).
3. *Quilter's Journal* 3, no. 4 (Winter 1980/1981), p. 9.
4. Scioto Imhoff Danner, "Memoirs" (unpublished MS), El Dorado, Kansas, July 22, 1970, p. 21.
5. *Quilter's Journal* 2, no. 2 (Summer 1979), p. 4.
6. Cuesta Benberry, "Hatfield-McCoy Victory Quilt," *Quilters Journal* 2, no. 3 (Fall 1979), pp. 6-7.
7. Herbert and Marjorie Katz, *Museums U.S.A.* (New York: Doubleday, 1965), p. 190.
8. "What I See from New York," *The House Beautiful* (April 1930), p. 420.
9. Elsie de Wolfe, *The House in Good Taste* (New York: The Century Co., 1913), p. 214.
10. Ibid., p. 215.
11. Ibid., p. 21.
12. Interview with Sally Garoutte, July 11, 1984.
13. Cuesta Benberry, untitled article, *Quilter's Newsletter* (October 1979), p. 10.
14. Carrie Hall and Rose Kretsinger, *The Romance of the Patchwork Quilt in America* (Caldwell, Idaho: Caxton Printers, 1935), p. 7.
15. Ibid., p. 29.
16. Interview with Sue Ellen Meyer, who runs an oral history program in Missouri, May 26, 1984.
17. U.S. Department of Commerce, Bureau of the Census, *People of Rural America* (Washington, D.C.: U.S. Government Printing Office, 1968), table II-2, p. 21.
18. Interview with Ruth Snyder, June 18, 1984.
19. Hall and Kretsinger, *Romance of the Patchwork Quilt*, p. 46.
20. Ninon, "Women Are Taking Up Quilting Again," *Chicago Daily News*, 1933.
21. William Rush Dunton, Jr., M.D., *Old Quilts* (Catonsville, Md.: William Rush Dunton, 1947), pp. 1-3.
22. Ibid., p. 7.
23. Ibid., p. 10.
24. Interviews with Barbara Brackman and Louise Townsend, July 16, 1984.
25. Joyce Gross, "Lillian Walker," *Quilter's Journal* 15, no. 1 (Spring 1981), pp. 1-3, 12-13.
26. "Betty Harriman," *Quilter's Journal* 1, no. 6 (Winter 1978), pp. 1-3.
27. Barbara Brackman, "The Great Chicago Quilting Bee of 1933," *Quilter's Journal*, no. 27 (July 1985), p. 16.
28. *Quilter's Newsletter*, no. 32 (June 1972), p. 10.
29. Ibid.
30. *Quilter's Newsletter* 4, no. 8 (August 1973), pp. 20-21.
31. Lilian Baker Carlisle, *Quilts at the Shelburne Museum* (Shelburne, Vt.: Shelburne Museum Publication, 1957), p. 58.
32. Interview with Louise Townsend.
33. Elizabeth King, untitled article on appliqué, *Quilting* (Leisure League of America, 1934), pp. 34-37. See also *Quilter's Newsletter*, no. 15 (January 1971), p. 4.
34. *Quilter's Newsletter* (February 1978), p. 23; (March 1976), p. 19.
35. Alain Lesieutre, *Art Nouveau* (New York: Paddington Press, 1974), p. 14, 37n.
36. Ibid.
37. Ruth E. Finley, *Old Patchwork Quilts and the Women Who Made Them* (Philadelphia and London: J. B. Lippincott, 1929), pp. 74-75.
38. Cuesta Benberry, "More Patriotic Quilts of the World War II Era," *Nimble Needle Treasures* (Sapulpa, Okla.) (Winter/December 1970).
39. Benberry, "Hatfield-McCoy Victory Quilt," pp. 6-7.
40. Cuesta Benberry, "Twentieth Century Game Plan: Naming the Quilt Pattern," *Quilter's Journal* 1, no. 2 (Winter 1977), p. 10.
41. Interview with Barbara Brackman.
42. Joyce Gross, "Pine Hawkes Eisfeller," *Quilter's Journal* 3, no. 4 (Winter 1980/81), p. 1.
43. Ibid., pp. 2-3.
44. Interview with Anna Chaney, July 17, 1984.
45. *Quilter's Newsletter* 5-6, no. 56 (June 1974), p. 4.
46. Interviews with Cuesta Benberry and Ruth Snyder, June 18, 1984.
47. Danner, "Memoirs," pp. 27-28.
48. Interview with Barbara Brackman.
49. Ibid.
50. Cuesta Benberry, "Quilt Kits—Past and Present, Part II," *Nimble Needle Treasures* 6, no. 4 (December 1974).
51. Hall and Kretsinger, *Romance of the Patchwork Quilt*, p. 17.
52. Ibid., p. 28.
53. *Quilter's Journal* 4, no. 1 (Spring 1981), pp. 4, 15.
54. Barbara Brackman, "Patterns from the 1933 Chicago World's Fair," *Quilter's Newsletter* (July/August 1981), p. 18.
55. Brackman, "Looking Back at the Great Quilt Contest," p. 23.
56. Brackman, "Patterns from the 1933 Chicago World's Fair," pp. 18-19.
57. Ibid.
58. "1940 New York World's Fair Quilt Contest and Exhibit," *Quilter's Journal* 3, no. 2 (Summer 1980), p. 14.
59. "Bertha Stenge," *Quilter's Journal* 2, no. 2 (Summer 1979), p. 3.
60. Interview with Cuesta Benberry.
61. Marie D. Webster, *Quilts: Their Story and How to Make Them* (New York: Doubleday, Page, 1915), p. 107.
62. *Quilter's Newsletter* (March 1980), p. 9.
63. Webster, *Quilts: Their Story*, pp. 96-97.
64. Hall and Kretsinger, *Romance of the Patchwork Quilt*, p. 15.

65. Ibid.
66. Finley, *Old Patchwork Quilts*, p. 128.
67. Hall and Kretsinger, *Romance of the Patchwork Quilt*, p. 15.
68. Ibid., p. 140.
69. "Journal of a Quiltmaker," *Quilter's Journal* 3, no. 3 (Fall 1980), p. 16.
70. Hall and Kretsinger, *Romance of the Patchwork Quilt*, p. 34.
71. Florence Peto, *Historic Quilts* (New York: American Historical Co., 1939), p. 193.
72. Webster, *Quilts: Their Story*, p. 129.
73. Finley, *Old Patchwork Quilts*, pp. 194–96.
74. Cuesta Benberry, "The Paradox of the Sunbonnet Girl Quilt Pattern," *Quilter's Journal* 2, no. 1 (Spring 1979), p. 12.
75. Patricia Almy, ed., *Nimble Needle Treasures* 6, no. 6 (March 1974).
76. Interview with Barbara Brackman.
77. Telephone interview with Pearl Thate, July 11, 1984.
78. Webster, *Quilts: Their Story*, p. 4.
79. Peto, *Historic Quilts*, p. 129.
80. Ibid.
81. Ibid., p. 132.
82. Ibid., p. 37.
83. Webster, *Quilts: Their Story*, pp. 46–48.
84. *Modern Priscilla* (October 1928), pp. 6–7.
85. *American Home Magazine* (November 1937), p. 27.
86. Rita Reif, "At Auction in 1983: Twentieth Century Soars," *The New York Times*, January 12, 1984.
87. Sears, Roebuck and Company, *1902 Catalog*, p. 764.
88. Barbara Brackman, *Encyclopedia of Pieced Quilt Patterns* (Lawrence, Kans.: Prairie Flower Publications, 1983), vol. 1, p. 1.
89. Linda Shogren, *The Quilt Pattern Index* (San Mateo, Calif.: Pieceful Pleasures Publishers, 1981).

# A GALLERY OF TWENTIETH CENTURY QUILTS

# FLOWERS THAT BLOOM IN THE SPRING

28. "Indiana Wreath." Emporia, Kansas. Signed and dated Rose G. Kretsinger, January 1927. 88" x 85". Marie D. Webster's original book frontispiece, a Hartford, Indiana, quilt dated 1858, served as the design source for this delightful appliqué spread. Mrs. Kretsinger achieved perfection with her keen sense of composition and restraint, with reverse appliqué and stuffed-work details adding to the overall immense appeal of this fine piece. (Collection of Spencer Museum of Art, The University of Kansas; Gift of Mary Kretsinger)

29. "Hollyhocks and Bluebirds." Ca. 1930. Found in Missouri. Cotton sateen. 88" x 78". Unlike most floral quilts that rely on repeated patterns, here a single story is told, as if the designer somehow knew quilts would be enjoyed as wall hangings later in the twentieth century. The blue grid creates the feeling of a paned window, overlooking a garden where bluebirds circle sweetly in the morning sun. A more traditional bedspread arrangement of hollyhocks was offered by Stearns & Foster's pattern #49. Photograph courtesy Karey Bresenhan. (Collection of Helen Pearce O'Bryant)

30. "Spring Tulips." 86" x 86". Made from a pattern offered by *Capper's Weekly* of Topeka, Kansas, this quilt has an added attraction. Picket fences provided suitable borders for a number of twentieth-century quilts, so the maker chose to add one to this tulip patch. Considering the proportions of the pickets, the tulips with their knotted stems in corsage arrangements would certainly garner ribbons at the county fair. Shell quilting adds rhythm and a sense of tilled soil to the white background, with touches of green suggesting grass edging. (Private collection)

31. "Field of Daisies." Ca. 1930. 78" x 64". Although the quilt was made from an Old Chelsea Station Needlecraft Service mail-order pattern, the color choices make a simple design striking. Yellow-centered flowers, perched on green stems, are so stylized as to lose their strictly botanical shape. Set against a distinctive 1930s orange-pink background, they seem more like setting suns, bonneted with blue rays. Photograph courtesy Carol Shope.

32. "Morning Glory." Ca. 1925. 82" x 72". Strictly for the exceptional needleworker, this pattern that is similar to one by Marie Webster, provided a showcase for fine quilting and difficult-to-appliqué details—delicate curving vines of flowers with circular knots at their stems. This is a blue-ribbon effort for the nearest county fair. (Private collection)

33. "Nosegay." Ca. 1935. 88" x 58". Having the old-fashioned charm of a banana split, this pattern made its debut in the very urban *New York Daily News*. It was sold under the auspices of Grandmother's Quilt Patterns, Book 22, pattern #2. Quilt columns, one of the most popular newspaper features of the 1930s, held their own even in New York. For 10¢ one could order a similar pattern called "Old Fashioned Nosegay," from the *Indianapolis Star*, 82 Eighth Avenue, New York City. That pattern was actually #486 from Laura Wheeler, the syndicate whose quilt designs were run by a number of newspapers nationwide. Inclusion of the local newspaper's name on the order blank made the quilt pattern seem as if it had come from its staff needlework editors. Photograph courtesy Noreen Lewandowski.

34. "Country Gardens." Ca. 1935. 98" x 82". Although it looks more like a skyscraper of window boxes, Stearns & Foster named its pattern #83 "Country Gardens," explaining that it was "a modern interpretation of a lovely country garden with flowers of many shades." The quiltmaker, against company advice, planted her "garden" with flowers of all the same shades, adding extra stylization. She did accede to the specified quilting pattern, which called for round bouquets on the non-floral blocks. Photograph courtesy Stearns & Foster.

35. "Mosaic Roses." Ca. 1935. 82" x 64". This computer-print-out-style quilt was the trademark of Ann Orr, *Good Housekeeping*'s needlework editor who launched her own pattern business. Stearns & Foster of Cincinnati offered its own version, "Roses are Red," pattern #66 in *An Album of Mountain Mist Quilt Blocks* (1938). It is unlikely that pattern designers in the 1930s could have predicted that the 1980s would bring us patterns actually designed by state-of-the-art computers, as recently exhibited by the Japanese in Tokyo. Photograph courtesy Joe Sarah. (Collection of Marna Wilson)

36. "Cross-stitch Garden." 82" x 74". Geometric florals composed of tiny square patches were very typical of Ann Orr's patterns, although this design was offered by Stearns & Foster, #42 in its Mountain Mist catalogues. Billed as a "new idea in quilting" that "transfers the technique of cross-stitch embroidery to the art of quilting," the style succeeds in the difficult task of creating floral motifs using no curvilinear patches. (Colletion of Eve Stuart)

37. "Painted Flowers." Ca. 1935. 82" x 78". Kits for painting quilts were widely advertised but relatively few are in existence now. Certainly their scarcity may be due to the skill required both to paint within a delicate pattern such as this one and to shade the colors for the pansies, morning glories, and other detailed flowers. Arranged in a traditional grid, each bouquet was painted on a fabric square, as were the individual yellow flowers. The blocks were then pieced with background squares and yellow corner blossoms to complete the spread. Photograph courtesy Merry Silber. (Private collection)

38. "Windblown Tulips." Ca. 1925. 78" x 80". Marie D. Webster illustrated this pattern in *Quilts: Their Story and How to Make Them* published in 1915. Two typically Dutch motifs—the tulip and the spinning windmill—have been combined in this popular appliqué pattern. The nine wheels of flowers seem to be stirring up a substantial breeze, for the tulips on the border are showing the effects of a strong spring wind. (Private collection)

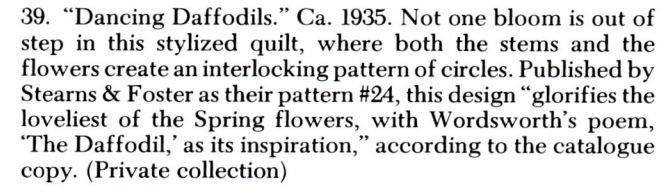

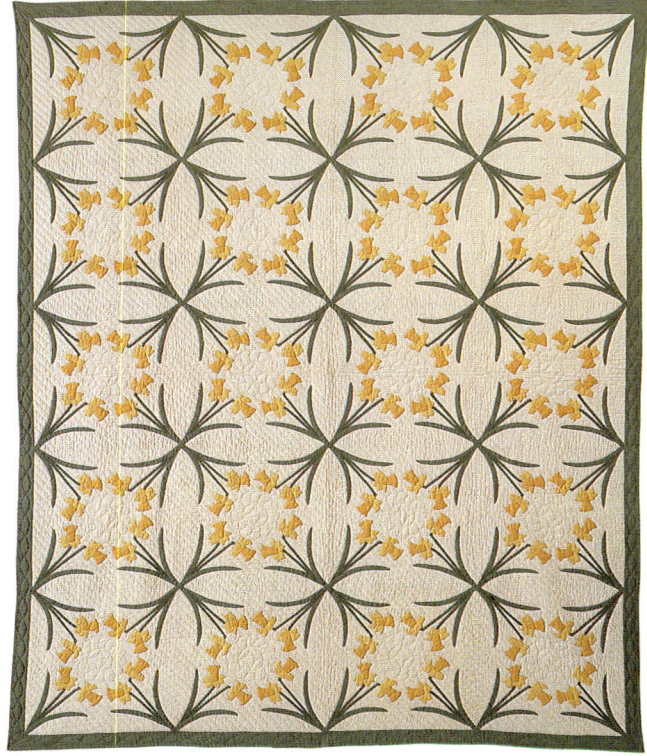

39. "Dancing Daffodils." Ca. 1935. Not one bloom is out of step in this stylized quilt, where both the stems and the flowers create an interlocking pattern of circles. Published by Stearns & Foster as their pattern #24, this design "glorifies the loveliest of the Spring flowers, with Wordsworth's poem, 'The Daffodil,' as its inspiration," according to the catalogue copy. (Private collection)

40. "Flowers and Lattice." Ca. 1935. 92" x 78". The appliquéd lattice, which supports this quilt's showiest blooms, adds an unusual graphic element to its design. The commercial-pattern flowers are sweet and simplified, as if picked from a lady's dress print rather than from a garden. (Collection of Lanford Wilson)

41. "Tree of Life." Pine Hawkes Eisfeller. 1939. A number of twentieth-century quilters were capable of producing workmanship that rivals the best of any preceding era. Pine Hawkes Eisfeller was a quilter of such stature that three of her spreads, including this one, garnered prizes in the hotly contested 1942 *Woman's Day* competition. Her inspiration for "Tree of Life" was a seventeenth-century Persian quilted bath carpet at the Victoria & Albert Museum in London. Mrs. Eisfeller found it on page 32 of Marie Webster's *Quilts: Their Story and How to Make Them* (1915). Photograph courtesy *Quilter's Newsletter Magazine*.

42. "Blue Iris." Made by Dr. Jeannette Dean Throckmorton (1883-1963). Des Moines, Iowa. Inscribed: "1945—Dr. Jeannette." 97⅞" x 72⅜". Midwestern quilters have contributed significantly to America's favorite folk art, as seen in this fine example by "Dr. Jeannette." The skill required to execute quilts of this quality is of the highest level, and the iris blooms in bold stuffed work highlight the wonderful quality of this beautiful piece. Courtesy the Art Institute of Chicago.

43. "Baby Chrysanthemum." Ca. 1934. 88" x 72". Like many commercial patterns, this stylized appliqué shows that designers for the leading syndicates were attuned to the latest style trends. However, the company preferred a "down-home" image, as seen in the copy that went along with this pattern. Offered as design #58 by Nancy Cabot, when it was published in the *Chicago Tribune* on February 7, 1934, it was billed as "one of the youngest in the quilt family and, with its extreme individuality, it is destined to go far." Photograph courtesy Noreen Lewandowski.

44. "Grapevine." Ca. 1930. 82" x 72". One factor contributing to the collectibility of softly hued pieces like this grapevine quilt is the resurgence of pastels as a popular decorating scheme. This textile confection has unusual embroidered veins on the leaves and stuffed-work grapes. (Private collection)

45. "Tulips." Ca. 1940. Nebraska. 98" x 78". Spring is truly bursting out all over in this bouyant pattern from a syndicated newspaper column using the names Laura Wheeler and Alice Brooks. Remarkable for its cheerful colors, it is enhanced by an unusual quilting treatment. Rather than being stitched with an overall pattern, each block features a snug halo of stitchery accenting each flower. The leaves all have quilted veins, and rows of contour quilting outline each lively motif. (Collection of Mr. and Mrs. Robert Steinberg)

46. "Bouquet of Pansies." Ca. 1935. 84" x 74". The proof that creating a lifelike pansy is a difficult task lies in these exraordinarily detailed flowers. Not only do some blossoms contain fourteen appliquéd patches in six different colors but they are also embellished with embroidery that adds shading as well as pistils and stamens. Even the leaves, made in three colors of green, have embroidered veining. (Private collection)

47. "Water Lilies." Midwestern U.S.A. Ca. 1938. 92" x 75". Stearns & Foster created pattern #47 for quilters who were skilled in the appliqué technique. Here is a fine example of a pattern enabling a talented needleworker to create an attractive quilt without having to possess advanced drawing and/or design skills. (Collection of Donna and Bryce Hamilton)

48. Floral appliqué with pieced borders. Ca. 1940. 80" x 78". This quilt is an exercise in floral geometry, rather than the randomness of nature. Its cheerful poinsietta-like blooms are carefully laid out so they form an X in the center, a counterpoint to the strong square lines of the double border of stripes. The quilting emphasizes yet another shape—circles interlocked like "Double Wedding Rings." (Private collection)

49. "Iris." Ca. 1938. 87" x 81". Variations in pattern "R" from Stearns & Foster could be made in various ways: connecting the "bases" of the flowers with diagonal strips, creating an overall hexagonal mosaic effect, or, as in this example, simplifying the top row of motifs by eliminating the blossoms, and adding a vertical row of flowers to widen the quilt. The company urged its customers to seek individuality in selecting colors, material, and design. (Collection of Maura and Lee Blumenthal)

50. "American Beauty Bouquet." Ca. 1935. 86" x 74". The kit for this quilt could be purchased from the Gold Art Needlework Company or from Lee Wards of Elgin, Illinois. A rose is a rose—except when it comes to quilting. Here each petal of these roses has been painstakingly appliquéd in four shades of pink to provide the realism and romance of garden blooms. Lest anyone consider the quiltmaker's vision to be purely sentimental, it should be noted that she carefully appliquéd green thorns on the brown stems of this appealing pattern quilt.

51. "Sweet Peas." Dated March 4, 1937. 76" x 56". Stearns & Foster's pattern #37 served as a guideline for a number of particularly appealing appliqué quilts, which could be rearranged to suit the maker. One Ohio State Fair prize winner, Mrs. Effie Van Meter of West Portsmouth, alternated her appliqué blocks with fancy quilted white blocks; another variation could be achieved by turning the crossed flower motifs on the diagonal. (Collection of Ruth Weeks)

52. "Iris Garland." Made by Hannah Haynes Headlee. Ca. 1938. Topeka, Kansas. 87" x 77". Although these irises appear to be blooming naturally, they actually form a perfect horseshoe. For their petals the artist used ten shades of purple—the darkest of which she dyed herself—plus three shades of yellow or orange. Photograph courtesy Marie Shirer. (Private collection)

53. "Flowers in a Vase." Made by Emma Mary Martha Andres. Prescott, Arizona. Ca. 1930. 72" x 55". Emma Andres was inspired by magazines and newspapers that brought the world to her in her small hometown where she worked in her father's cigar store. While previous generations of quilters relied on more direct handing down of ideas and patterns from mother to daughter, twentieth-century quilters found a wealth of inspiration from periodicals like *Woman's World*, from which Miss Andres ordered a "Tiger Lily" quilt kit. Thus began her love affair with quilting, which produced a number of outstanding pieces. Photograph courtesy Laurene Sinema.

54. "Roses." Ca. 1930. Although the floral motifs appear to be growing with random exuberance, they are all carefully planned. The branch configuration in the top left corner, for example, is repeated in the bottom right. Similarly, the other two corners and the center branches are mirror images. The flowers are skillfully executed with two shades of pink and embroidered details, as suggested by the pattern company's directions.

55. "Urn of Flowers." Ca. 1925. 38¾" x 35½". This classical vase with its imaginative appliquéd and embroidered flowers was created as the central motif for a quilt that was never completed. (Private collection)

56. Floral appliqué with embroidery. Ca. 1935. By combining appliqué and embroidery, a quilter could achieve large colored blooms plus curling tendrils, ribbons, and intricately detailed petals. This commercial pattern was executed by a skilled needleworker fond of colorful morning glories, roses, and pansies. (Private collection)

57. American Calico cross-stitch embroidered quilt. Ca. 1945. Newport, Rhode Island. 88" x 62". Pennsylvania Dutch motifs in this commercial kit from the Paragon Pattern Company, N.Y., can be seen in its stylized tulips and roses, as well as in the classic reds, yellows, and greens used in its elaborate embroidery. Photograph courtesy Capt. Tryon Antiques, New York.

58. "Pots of Flowers." Ca. 1930. Pennsylvania. 88" x 82". Cut flowers, as anyone knows, need water. Thus these red and yellow blooms are all set in vases—even those on the border. Abloom with berries and heart-like buds, they shelter several very sprightly red birds. The flatness of the floral arrangements, which almost seem to be cut from paper, is reminiscent of Egyptian decorative art popular in the twentieth century. The quilting, with wreaths and flowers, is expecially fine in this reinterpretation of a traditional motif. (Private collection)

59. "Oriental Poppy." Ca. 1930. 82" x 76". Ruby S. McKim's Studios in Independence, Missouri, offered this mail-order pattern #380C with all of the pieces ready cut for $4.50, or the pattern only, #380, for 20 cents. Her 1920s and 1930s designs often had a stylized, fragmented style with unique, zesty appeal. (Private collection)

60. "Pinwheel Sunflower." Ca. 1935. 97" x 81". Although the blossoms are rather "down home" in their cheery prints, their stems reflect sophisticated Art Deco angles. Finely quilted sunflowers add richness to the plain white background. Created by a professional artist or designer, here is a good example of the age-old practice of taking elements from old designs and dressing them in the latest fashions. Old Chelsea Station Needlecraft Service, which offered the pattern, also sold a stemless pinwheel design entitled "Wheel of Fortune." (Private collection)

61. "Tulip Garden." Pennsylvania. Ca. 1940. 89½" x 88". A chorus of spring-blooming tulips greets us with a joyful salute to irrepressible optimists. (Private collection)

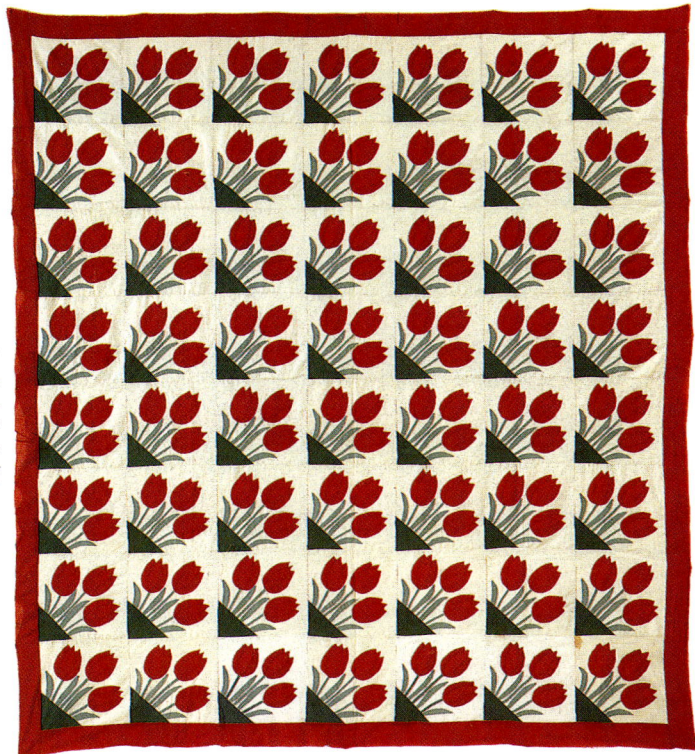

62. "Tulips." Appliqué and pieced top. Ca. 1930. 74″ x 64″. With flowers that seem to be literally bursting from the earth, this lively quilt top captures the exuberance of spring. However, its popular 1930s shades evoke a more wintery holiday season. For allusions to Christmas, red tulips may have been especially appropriate since they are the flowers of Christmas in Scandinavia. (Collection of Nora Ephron)

63. "Kansas Pattern." 1935. Made by Charlotte Jane Whitehill. 94″ x 91″. The pattern for this quilt was borrowed from Mrs. S. J. Soden of Emporia, Kansas, but was executed with a significant change: the center circle of appliquéd flowers was reproduced instead with fine quilting stitchery, lending an overall lightness and understated grace to the spread. (Collection of The Denver Art Museum)

64. "Cottage Garden." Ca. 1935. 82″ x 82″. Quilter Pine Eisfeller, stationed in Hawaii with her husband from 1930 to 1935, and strongly influenced by Hawaiian quilts, was inspired by an 1857 floral appliqué made by Arsinoe Kelsey Bowen of Maryland. She entered her quilts in the 1942 *Woman's Day* National Needlework contest, won second Grand Prize, and the magazine adapted her quilt for a pattern to sell to its readers. This splendid example belongs to the Eisfeller style, and it rivals the best work of previous generations of quilters. (Collection of Edwin Binney III and Gail Binney-Winslow)

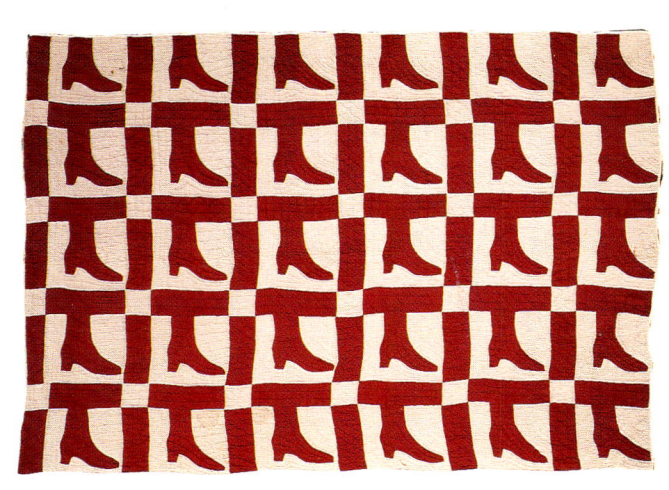

# OBJECTS OF MY AFFECTION

65. "Lady's Boot." Ca. 1890. Kentucky. 68" x 95". This well-heeled Victorian quilt, made from an 1890s pattern in Kentucky, is an amusing precursor of the early twentieth-century silhouette quilt, in which a mundane object is endlessly repeated. Ruth Finley, in *Old Patchwork Quilts* (1929), was not enthusiastic about this somewhat unusual genre. In the twentieth century, however, quilts with mundane objects in a repeated pattern became popular, and are now considered very collectible as examples of textile Pop Art. (Collection of Cuesta Benberry)

66. "Indians." Early twentieth century. Pennsylvania. 80" x 66". This Indian motif, inspired by a weathervane, sports an almost Egyptian profile, complete with eyes outlined in black. A loose border of triangles edges both the interior and exterior sides of the rectangles. (Collection of Mr. and Mrs. Howard T. Barnett)

67. "Trees." Ca. 1925. 84" x 66". These trees have a naive charm all their own, from the conelike trunks to the heavily laden branches. Obviously fertile, their generic red fruits are three-dimensional, appliquéd balls. Photograph courtesy Betty Sterling. (Collection of Jo A. Wood)

68. "Umbrella" quilt top. Ca. 1935. 70" x 70". Perhaps the maker of this quilt top was saving it for a rainy day. Her umbrella appliqués, executed in the popular red and green duo, were never backed or quilted. Photograph courtesy Beverly Labe.

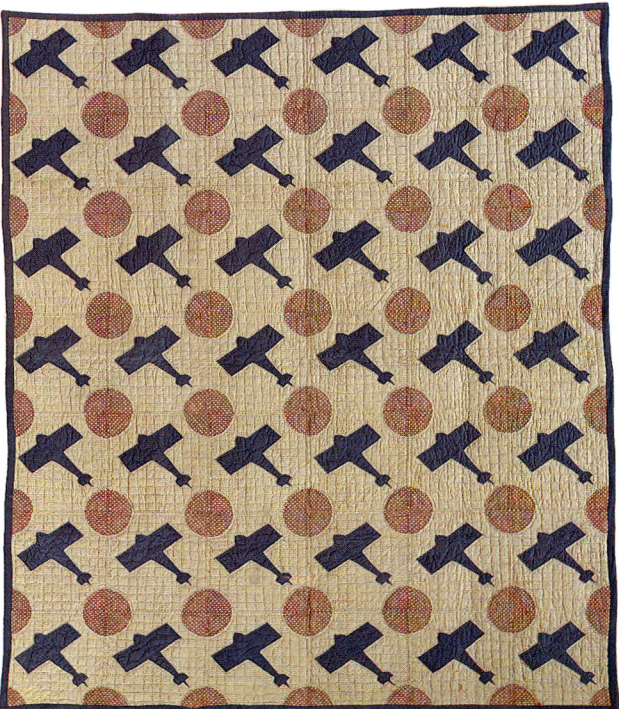

69. "Coffee Cups." Ca. 1940. 84" x 74". Everyday objects like cups occasionally did runneth over in twentieth-century quilt design. This pattern, offered by the *Kansas City Star* in 1935 as "Coffee Cups" and in 1946 as "The Cup and Saucer," provided the quiltmaker wth a homey way to display a host of choice fabric scraps. (Collection of Joanna S. Rose)

70. "Airplanes." Ca. 1930. 78" x 66". Mothers, responding to decorating advice in the mazagines, were always searching for quilt motifs suitable for boys' rooms. In the age of popular hero Charles Lindbergh, the airplane was a fine solution. Here it is appliquéd in periwinkle blue, the protypical 1930s color. (Collection of Beverly Swihart)

71. "Trolley Cars." Ca. 1910. New England. 84" x 79". The clang! of these patchwork streetcars makes one nostalgic for an era when one sang songs about romance, picnics, and meeting at the fair in St. Louis. Photograph courtesy Bettie Mintz.

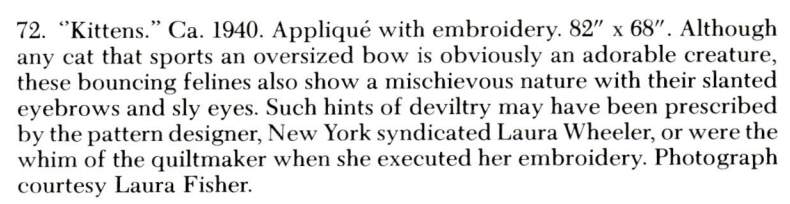

72. "Kittens." Ca. 1940. Appliqué with embroidery. 82" x 68". Although any cat that sports an oversized bow is obviously an adorable creature, these bouncing felines also show a mischievous nature with their slanted eyebrows and sly eyes. Such hints of deviltry may have been prescribed by the pattern designer, New York syndicated Laura Wheeler, or were the whim of the quiltmaker when she executed her embroidery. Photograph courtesy Laura Fisher.

73. Butterflies. 1930–1940. Appliqué with embroidery. 80" x 68". Made in Fayette City, Alabama. Diving toward pink tulips, these butterflies have an almost Oriental quality. The black shadows strikingly emphasize the color and pattern of the butterflies' wings. (Collection of Helen and Robert Cargo)

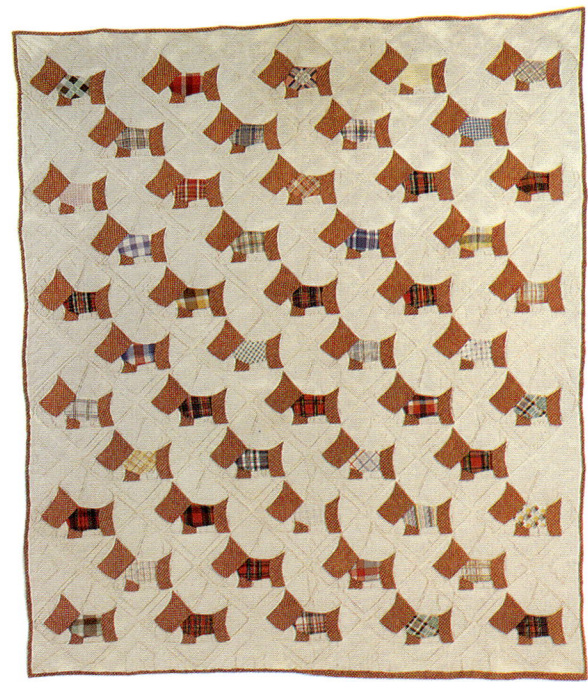

74. "Scotties." Ca. 1935. 79" x 66". Alice Brooks, a New York syndicated columnist, offered pattern #5673 to fans of President Roosevelt's Scottie, Fala. As individuals, these sporty dogs, each with a carefully chosen plaid coat, are typical of the homey motifs that appealed to 1930s quilters. However, as a group they create a graphic collage of Art Deco angles and curves that is surprisingly sophisticated. (Collection of Rochelle Epstein)

75. "Dicky Bird." Ca. 1930. Appliqué with embroidery. 72" x 70". These appealing birds, all warbling atop their houses, were made from a Laura Wheeler pattern, offered in newspapers for 20 cents. Because "Needlework by Laura Wheeler" was a major syndicated column, the pattern doubtless appeared in a number of papers; however, we have not seen another example of this charming pattern completed. Photograph courtesy Kelter-Malcé Antiques. (Collection of Marsha and Jay Mendel)

76. "Pine Trees." Ca. 1930. 88" x 70". The tree motif has a long history in quilting, from the early Tree of Life to this stylized, twentieth-century pine forest from the Alice Brooks/Laura Wheeler syndicate. Made from a pattern, this pieced evergreen design was offered, with minor variations, by at least one other company. (Private collection)

77. "Turtles." Ca. 1910. 73½" x 63". Thirty red turtles with bulging stuffed heads and tails *and* bright button eyes may not win any beauty contests, but they certainly make a statement in this quilt. Robbing-Peter-to Pay-Paul, possibly the design basis for this oddly amusing creation, was never like this. (Collection of Robert Bishop)

# ROUND AND ROUND

78. "Double Wedding Ring." Ca. 1935. 86" x 68". Bridal white was naturally the more common background color choice for "Double Wedding Ring" quilts, one reason why this example with its pleasing blue background is so striking. The energy of its busy print rings would perhaps pale against a less assertive color. (Private collection)

79. "Rainbow Double Wedding Ring." Ca. 1935. 85" x 74". Like the lights moving around a movie marquee, the "Double Wedding Ring" with its circles of dancing color, is a twentieth-century phenomenon. It is indisputably one of the three most popular post-1900 quilt designs. Because its rings required careful piecing, it served in many ways as the hallmark of a skillful quiltmaker. Fine examples are clearly set off from the mundane by unusual color choice—in this case all solids—and elaborate quilting, and are cherished as wedding gifts by present-day romantics. (Private collection)

80. "Pickle Dish." Ca. 1935. 85" x 60". Always a pattern that evokes swirling motion, the "Double Wedding Ring" is given a rhythmic boost with Sawtooth or Pickle Dish triangular patterning. A scalloped edge, more difficult to execute, makes the circular motif even more prominent, as does the quilting—rings within rings on the white background. Home Art Studios of Des Moines, Iowa, offered this pattern, although with a different quilting design, as "Indian Wedding Ring," available free with the purchase of their 32-page Colonial Quilt Book, for 25 cents. Photograph courtesy Kelter-Malcé Antiques.

81. "Double Wedding Ring." Amish. Ca. 1925. Atlantic, Pennsylvania. 85″ x 66½″. Twentieth-century Amish quilt makers sometimes used quilt patterns belonging to their "English" (non-Amish) neighbors, reinterpreting them in their own distinctive colors, using all solids. The results were sometimes startling, dramatic renditions of a relatively common pattern. (Museum of American Folk Art)

82. "Friendship Wheel." Dated 1915. Wool. 80″ x 80″. Probably sewn to mark a marriage or anniversary, this Friendship quilt is a free-wheeling family tree. "Father & Mother" is embroidered in the bull's eye of the central block; children's names along with two sets of grandparents, the Hengsts and the Colebaughs, surround them. At the center of the other blocks are the names of aunts and uncles, with their children orbiting on the other patches. (Private collection)

70

83. "Friendship Fans." Ca. 1932. Lincoln, Nebraska. 108" x 72". This fan quilt was made at the East Lincoln Christian Church. The church members paid 25¢ to have their names embroidered on the quilt, which was then raffled. A descendent of the person who won the quilt in the raffle donated the quilt back to the church in the early 1970s, at which time over half of the people whose names appear on the quilt were still members of the church. Photograph courtesy Doni Boyd.

84. "Fans." Ca. 1925. 94" x 80". These fans unfurl a sampling of favorite 1920s colors. However, their inherent gaiety is given an unexpectedly restrained counterpoint by the distinctive tan background, a color not often chosen by quilters of any era. Unusual, too, is the outlining on the fans, as dark and dramatic as the eyeliner of a Hollywood starlet. (Collection of Rochelle Epstein)

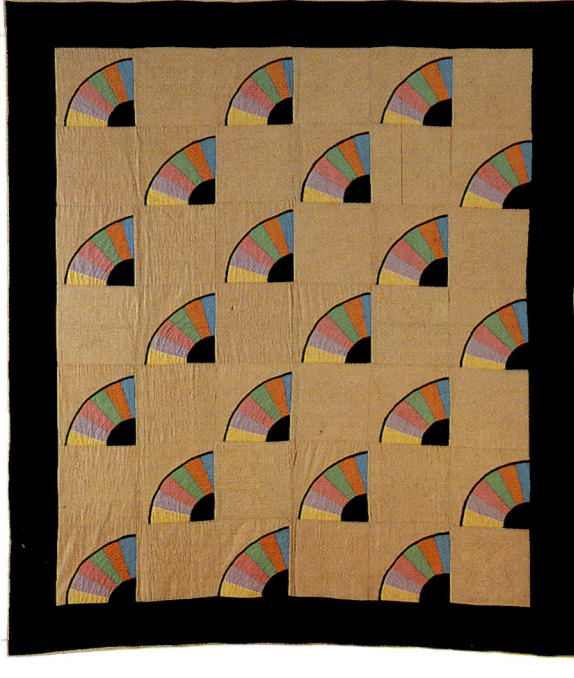

85. "Fans." Ca. 1930. 79" x 70". Pieced with white between each fold, these fans seem more like setting suns, their rays splayed out against white mountains. Each fan is quilted in a rainbow pattern; its background is quilted with vertical stripes. The angular edge of the quilt, punctuated by pink quarter-suns, enhances the vitality of this version of a favorite pattern. (Private collection)

86. "Fans." Ca. 1930. Michigan. 84" x 74". The rainbow stripes of these fans combine to create long diagonal swirls rather like the tresses of a silent-film star, or perhaps an Art Deco goddess who would adorn a cinema ceiling. The tips of the fans are pieced, but the candy-colored stripes are appliquéd. The border is quilted with a series of rays emanating from unseen suns. Photograph courtesy Sandra Mitchell.

87. "Gypsy Trail"/"Snake in the Hollow." Ca. 1930. Michigan. 82″ x 72″. The singing and dancing of the roaring twenties are suggested in this rhythmic piece. The black tips of its fans, set against white, form bow ties. Repeated, the image evokes a crowd of well-heeled young live wires assembled for a smashing party—and perhaps some foxtrotting. The key border adds a smashing Art Deco touch. Photograph courtesy Sandra Mitchell and Joan Townsend.

88. "Double Wedding Ring" being quilted. Transylvania, Louisiana. June 1940. The U.S. Department of Agriculture Security Administration labeled this photograph with a brief caption: "Mrs. Clarence N. Pace's mother-in-law quilting in their home." The picture says a great deal more, however, about the making of a quilt. Here is one of the most popular twentieth-century patterns in progress. Having been carefully pieced and now stretched over a quilting frame, the quilt top, batting, and backing are being sewn into a textile sandwich by fine quilt stitchery that serves two important functions: holding the layers together, and adding decorative details. The quilter's dress, incidentally, is of material typical of the period which, when no longer new, most likely would be recycled into a quilt by its thrifty owner's loving hands. (Library of Congress)

# SHINING STARS

89. "Eastern Star." Ca. 1935. 80" x 80". The medallion of the women's group, the Eastern Star, was a natural for quilters. This fine example, pattern #152 offered by Home Art Studios of Des Moines, Iowa, is notable for its elaborate quilting—hearts, for loyalty, fill the background, and each large triangle of solid color is quilted with a cup, sheaf of wheat, or other symbol. Photograph courtesy Betty Osband.

90. "Star of France." Ca. 1930. 79" x 78". Inspired by a military decoration of the Napoleonic era, this handsome design was pattern #151 from the Home Art Studios of Des Moines, Iowa. Although the use of four shades of yellow sateen was recommended, the pattern maker also noted that four shades of blue, orchid, or pink would also work well. (Private collection)

91. "Starburst." Ca. 1935. 71" x 75". The thousands of fabric diamonds that form the eight points of this star would be enough to mark any quilter as a virtuoso. However, the maker went one step further and pieced a galaxy of squares in a "Trip-Around-the-World" block for each of the four corners. Although executed with all the mastery of the nineteenth century, this quilt clearly has a twentieth-century sensibility with its cheerful pastels, arranged so that the star actually seems to shimmer with modern light. Photograph courtesy Sandra Mitchell. (Collection of Christi Finch)

92. "Broken Star." Ca. 1930. Midwestern Amish. 76" x 80". Although this pattern was published by a number of companies including Stearns & Foster, this dramatic example shows the distinctive coloring of the Amish of Ohio and Indiana. Practical by nature, the Amish were quick to borrow time-saving patterns from their "English" neighbors, although they usually reinterpreted them in their dark and distinctive rainbow of polished cottons. Here, the eight points of the central star seem to have ignited the night sky in a dazzling display of celestial fireworks. (Private collection)

93. "Compass and Wreath." Ca. 1935. Midwestern U.S.A. 88" x 80". The traditional Mariner's Compass is used here in an unusual twentieth-century treatment. Pieced in the center in two favorite Art Deco colors—red and black—it is bordered by a holiday wreath with a peach-colored appliqué bow; then it is framed with a garland of flowering vines, more typical of early nineteenth-century "Center Medallion" quilts. Finally, there is a strong red inner border with compass points in red and black, and an outer border of periwinkle blue, another favorite thirties color. Fine quilting is showcased on a white background in a serpentine feather pattern. Photograph courtesy Madeline Smith.

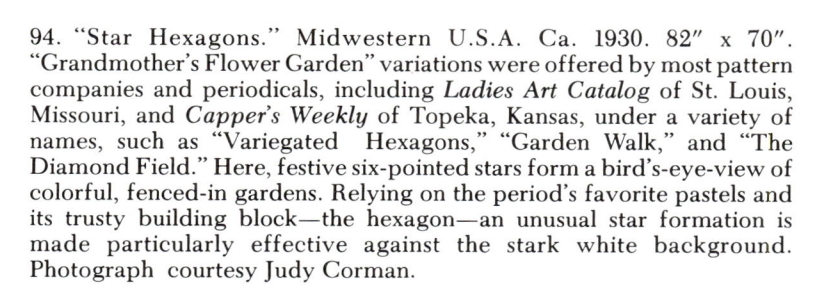

94. "Star Hexagons." Midwestern U.S.A. Ca. 1930. 82" x 70". "Grandmother's Flower Garden" variations were offered by most pattern companies and periodicals, including *Ladies Art Catalog* of St. Louis, Missouri, and *Capper's Weekly* of Topeka, Kansas, under a variety of names, such as "Variegated Hexagons," "Garden Walk," and "The Diamond Field." Here, festive six-pointed stars form a bird's-eye-view of colorful, fenced-in gardens. Relying on the period's favorite pastels and its trusty building block—the hexagon—an unusual star formation is made particularly effective against the stark white background. Photograph courtesy Judy Corman.

76

95. "Star of Bethlehem." Ca. 1930. 90" x 90". A number of commercial pattern companies and periodicals offered this Star design, including McKim Studios of Independence, Missouri, Home Art Studios of Des Moines, Iowa, and the *Rural New Yorker*, published in New York from 1841 through the mid-twentieth century. Executed here in fashionable "Tango" shades, and with a beautifully quilted background, the pattern was issued under such names as "Lone Star," "Star of the East," "Blazing Star," "Pride of Texas," "Rising Star," and, ultimately, "Star of Stars!" (Private collection)

96. "Carpenter's Wheel." 1949. Pieced by Katrin Raffety. Grinnell, Iowa. 84" x 74". Quilted by Charlene Oliver, ca. 1970. Our grandmother, at age 85, had numerous versions of this pattern from which to choose, offered by pattern companies and periodicals such as *People's Popular Monthly, Hearth and Home, Kansas City Star*, and Nancy Page syndicated columns, written by Florence LaGanke. A wide variety of names had been dreamed up, including "Diadem Star," "Lone Star of Paradise," "Black Diamond," and, inevitably, "Star Within a Star!" Photograph courtesy Frances W. Woodard.

97. "Starburst." Ca. 1940. Michigan. 82" x 66". This star quilt with its wonderful galaxy of prints is a perfect example of a scrap-bag quilt. Leftover bits of dresses and clothes were carefully pieced in a controlled composition of colorful blazing energy. On only one of the eight points of her star did the maker run short on fabric and combine two different fabrics with polka dots. Photograph courtesy Wild Goose Chase Quilt Gallery.

# A TISKET, A TASKET

98. "French Baskets." Signed and dated, "Agnata Voss—1930." 92" x 88". The pattern for this lacy basket quilt was originally designed in 1915 for *The Ladies' Home Journal* when Marie D. Webster was needlework editor. Later, when she left the magazine and went into the pattern business from her home in Marion, Indiana, she offered stamped kits for this quilt for $12.00. Basted versions were $37.50, and finished quilts, $50.00. In the 1930s, Mrs. Scioto Danner, who sold patterns from Kansas, offered the same "French Baskets," but changed the name to "The Ivory Basket," a pattern that sold nicely at 75¢. (Collection of Dana Alpern)

99. "Basket of Flowers," Ca. 1930. New Jersey 96" x 68". Quite unconventionally, the maker of this quilt chose black as the background for her appliqué quilt. Her intention may have been to make a memorial quilt, but more probably she just liked the dramatic color combination. Although midwestern Amish quiltmakers of the same period often chose black for the background color, it is most unlikely that this maker was influenced by the Amish, where appliqué was frowned upon by the truly devout. (Collection of Barbara Johnson)

100. "Basket of Roses." 1938. Made by Hannah Haynes Headlee. Topeka, Kansas. 84" x 71". Although the floral border of this quilt echoes the Art Nouveau tone of Mrs. Headlee's other quilts, her central basket of flowers owes its inspiration to another Kansas quilter, Rose Kretsinger, known for her floral appliqués. In Mrs. Headlee's hands, however, the flowers achieve a remarkable, lifelike shading—there is a hint of pink in the yellow roses, for example. Mrs. Headlee may either have painted the fabric or carefully chosen commercial prints with just the right subtle transition of hues. Her basket is realistically woven with green fabric strips. (Collection of Viola Shirer)

101. "Flower Baskets." Appliqué and pieced. Ca. 1930. 78" x 78". These four cheerful baskets, cleverly made with bias-cut candy-striped handles, hold perky lollipop flowers, edged in black accent stitching. The background boasts a host of quilted leaves and petals. (Private collection)

102. "Baskets of Flowers." Embroidered. Ca. 1930. With thread of only one color—the ever-popular periwinkle blue—this quiltmaker managed to assemble nine varieties of flowers, from daisies to roses, arranged in nine different baskets. It should be noted that an important period prop for the flower arranger was the ribbon bow, which festoons six of these squares. (Private collection)

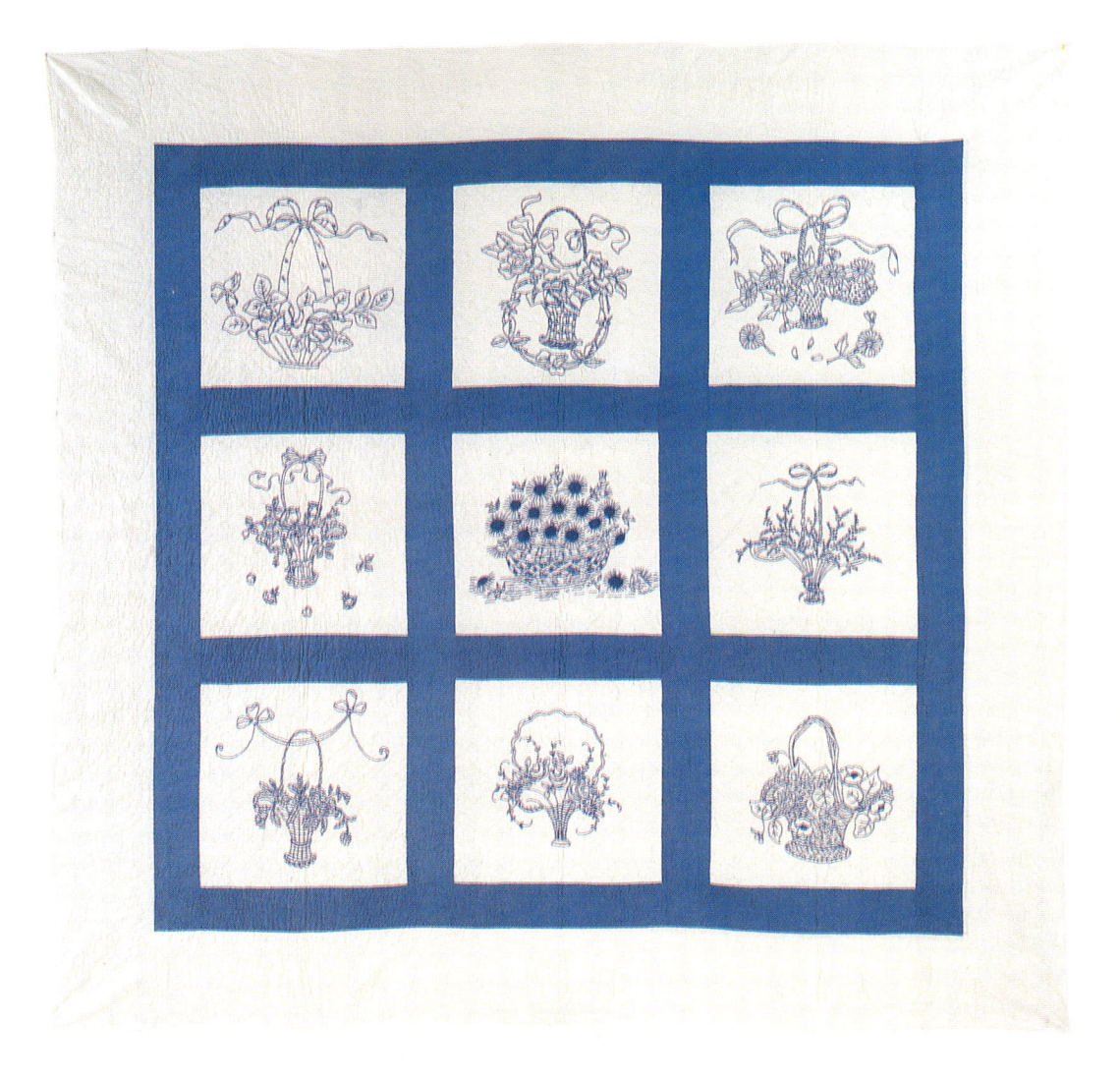

103. "Hexagon Baskets." Ca. 1940. 102" x 86". The building block for these baskets is the twentieth-century favorite, the hexagon, popular because of its ability to simulate petals. Although executed from a commercial pattern, this quilt did not offer the maker an easy way out. Its all-white background is composed of tiny hexagons of the same scale as the flower's petals. The bottom border of triangles created an interesting flourish for the foot of a bed. Photograph courtesy Madeline Smith.

104. "Checkboard Baskets." Ca. 1930. 76" x 66". These baskets of bright blooms show an inventive designer's eye—checkerboard squares to simulate a basket weave, and appliquéd circles to create the feeling of a lacy handle. The quilting pattern of sun rays, most likely specified by the pattern company, enhances the exuberance of this delightful pastiche. (Private collection)

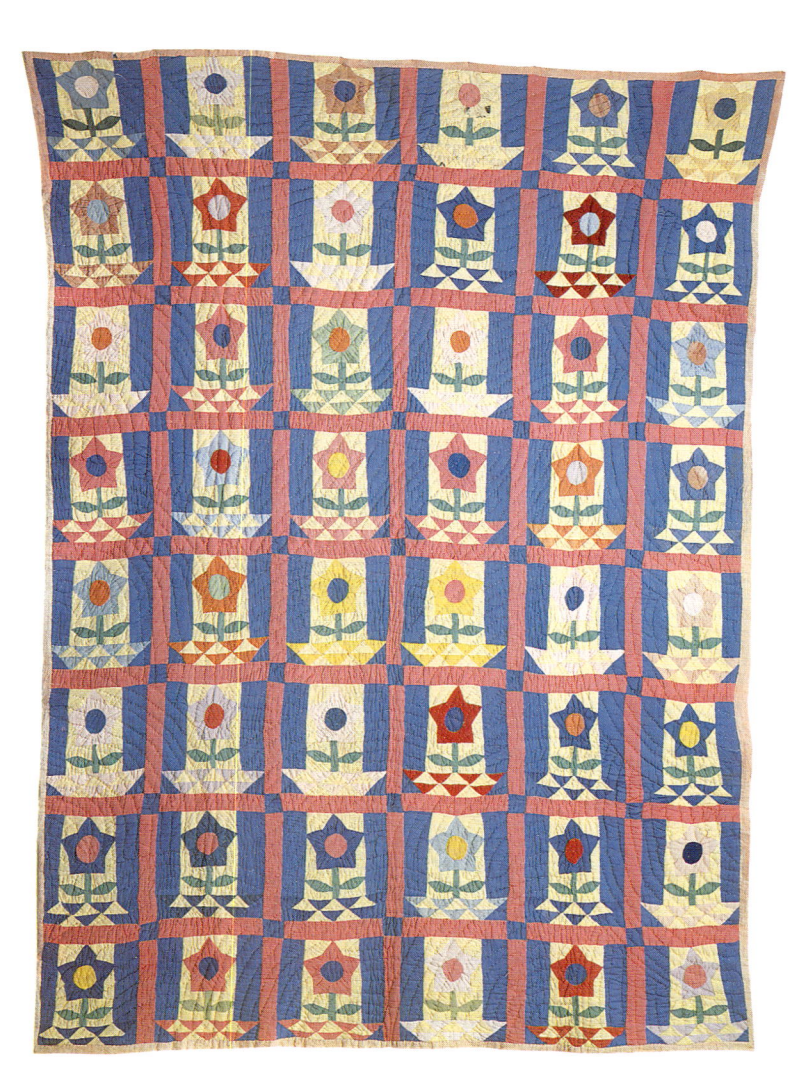

105. "Baskets of Star Flowers." Ca. 1935. 89" x 63". Large-scale Clamshell quilting was favored by some quilters of the rural South. Here the stitchery pattern sweeps through a field of wide-open blossoms greeting the day with a spirited song of good cheer. Photograph courtesy Laura Fisher.

# HOME SWEET HOME

106. "House-on-the-Hill." Ca. 1930. 89" x 70". The American dream of a home of one's own in a nice neighborhood is epitomized in this cheery appliqué community from the Alice Brooks/Laura Wheeler syndicate. A picket fence protects this dreamscape with its calico shrubs and trees and with a quilted path leading hospitably to the front door of each house. The pattern was described by its manufacturer as an appliqué suitable for youngsters' rooms. (Private collection)

107. "Schoolhouse." Ca. 1940. 89" x 66". This commercially designed Christmas-colored quilt was cleverly designed so that the schoolhouses are always right side up on the bed no matter which direction the viewer is facing. Its color scheme, a typical one for the period, appears on several similar quilts, perhaps because red is the quintessential color for schoolhouses and the most appropriate shade for lawns is, of course, green. Photograph courtesy Betty Osband.

108. "Log Cabin." Ca. 1930. 80" x 72". Although the split-rail fences create such lively frames in this quilt, the early years of the twentieth century was not a roaring time for all. As the lonely log cabin suggests, many women still lived isolated on the farm, and quilting bees, especially during the Depression, remained a major source of social life. Photograph courtesy Sandra Mitchell.

109. "Schoolhouse." Ca. 1930. Maryland. 77" x 66". Although the repeated schoolhouse motif could be considered a precursor of Pop Art, it is treated in a far from abstract manner in this quilt. Here the maker chose a log-like horizontal stripe for her walls and embellished her schoolhouses with a host of realistic detail: clamshell quilting that simulates shingles on the roof, quilted "panes" on all the windows and doors, and even a herringbone pattern to indicate a thriving lawn. She also softened the graphic red, white, and blue scheme by using pink "mortar" to join the walls and roofs. Photograph courtesy M. Finkel & Daughter.

110. "Honeymoon Cottage." Ca. 1935. 86" x 72". This pattern, which could be ordered by mail from Sears, Roebuck, shows a popular and basic form of twentieth-century housing. A mail-order pattern from Ruby Short McKim, these quilted bungalows look unexpectedly modern—large windows, a cozy fireplace, and a wide driveway. The paint colors—peach, green, navy blue—were fashionable colors for clothing in the thirties. (Private collection)

111. "Summer Time 1933." Inscribed and dated by Mrs. Noah Webster. The maker arranged elements of her favorite quilt patterns—houses, trees, tulips, birds, and urns from such syndicated patterns as Nancy Page's "Garden Bouquet"—with the easygoing spirit of her quilt's title. The houses, although randomly placed, all feature a blue windowshade, lending charm to this fond memory piece. (Collection of Diane and Clyde Brownstone)

85

112. "Cross-stitch Sampler." Ca. 1940. 96" x 66". Inspired by schoolgirls' art of the eighteenth and nineteenth centuries, this bed-size "sampler" displays the craft of cross-stitch embroidery that became widely popular again in the twentieth century. (Collection of Robert Bishop)

113. *Autumn Winds* by Andrée N. Ca. 1930. 17¾" x 23¼". Like the best of home sweet homes, this bungalow manages to be a stronghold of serenity in a blustery landscape. This painting, although more intense than the popular 1920s and 1930s house-quilt patterns, parallels quilting in its colors: the same orange, green, pink, and blue that were favorites in fabric. (Private collection)

114. Pre-stamped and embroidered pillow cover. Ca. 1930. 14" x 14½". Home is clearly where the heart is, according to this pillow cover. The influence of quilt motifs can be seen, especially in the garland of flowers. The whole piece, thanks to the careful embroidery, looks as if it had been appliquéd, instead of pre-tinted. (Private collection)

# PEOPLE AND PROGRESS

115. "Fashion Ladies." Ca. 1920. Appliqué with pieced border. 90" x 81". The full-skirted pose struck by this parade of women owes a very strong debt to Sunbonnet Sue of the late 1800s. However, a handful of these modern, twentieth-century women have subtly broken the mold. Several boast the latest in fashion—pajama pants—and two have turned to face the viewer: one to display her tennis serve and the other, walking her dog, to reveal a smartly made-up face beneath her bonnet. (Collection of Gerry Lou Silverman)

116. "Sunbonnet Sue." Ca. 1940. 94½" x 82". The rise and fall of Sue as a quilt motif has been well chronicled over the years, and she has even been the subject of some derision from time to time. In any case, she rises once again delightfully bandanaed in this unusually spunky, punchy version. Photograph courtesy Susan Parrish.

117. "Century of Progress". Dated 1833–1933. 82" x 70". To illustrate the idea of progress the theme of the 1933 Chicago fair, this quilter focused on transportation—from the stage coach and locomotive, both dated 1835, to the automobile and airplane of 1933. Building progress is represented by four blocks showing a log cabin, a country church, skyscrapers, and a large church. The futuristic building at the center is the Century of Progress building itself. The American eagle, a car and two locomotives are included in the exceptionally fine quilting. (Collection of Barbara Johnson)

118. "Century of Progress." Designed and pieced by Emma Mae Leonhard. Inscribed: "1833–1933." Virginia, Illinois. 85" x 75". The entrance form for the 1933 Chicago quilt contest is still attached to the lower left corner of this tour-de-force quilt. With houses juxtaposed against pastel skyscrapers plus a chronology of women's and military fashions, it charts a Century of Progress, as required by the contest guidelines. An English teacher, Miss Leonhard pointed out in her notes that she sacrificed historical exactness in terms of the colors she chose for the uniforms pictured in her quilt for the sake of "daintiness of the color scheme in the whole quilt." The evolution of transportation is also illustrated in the fine quilting in the top and bottom borders. Photograph courtesy Marie and Thomas Foster.

119. "World of Tomorrow." Made by Mrs. Pearl Willard Roberds of Olathe, Kansas. Designed by JoRo Betts of Washington, D.C. 94" x 78". Although this quilt looks as if it would have been a sure winner at the 1939 World's Fair, it was disqualified because it was 11 flags shy of the requisite 64, the number of nations in the world at that time. Mrs. Roberds, whose daughter had researched and designed 64 flags, hadn't been able to fit them all on. However, after her death, her daughter, Mrs. Betts, added the 11 missing flags. They can be seen flying on the crowded left side of the quilt. Despite its lack of World's Fair acclaim, this "World of Tomorrow" quilt was exhibited at Macy's department store in New York City and won a number of ribbons at Kansas fairs. "World's Fair 1939" is repeated in fine quilt stitches throughout the background. (Collection of Gay Imbach and Joyce Bacon)

120. "Women of All Nations." 1920. Painted Post, N.Y. Made by Ruth Easton Figaro. 102" x 78". A prize winner at the Century of Progress exposition, this quilt shows people of many countries, such as a Scotswoman demonstrating the highland fling, and a Swede on skis. An Eskimo stands in front of her igloo. Each delegate is labeled with an embroidered inscription, should one not recognize her native costume. Of course, the Indian and the Pilgrim, representing the U.S., are featured in the central square. Photograph courtesy Elizabeth Ingber. (Collection of Harriet and Bruce Blank)

# GRAPHICALLY SPEAKING

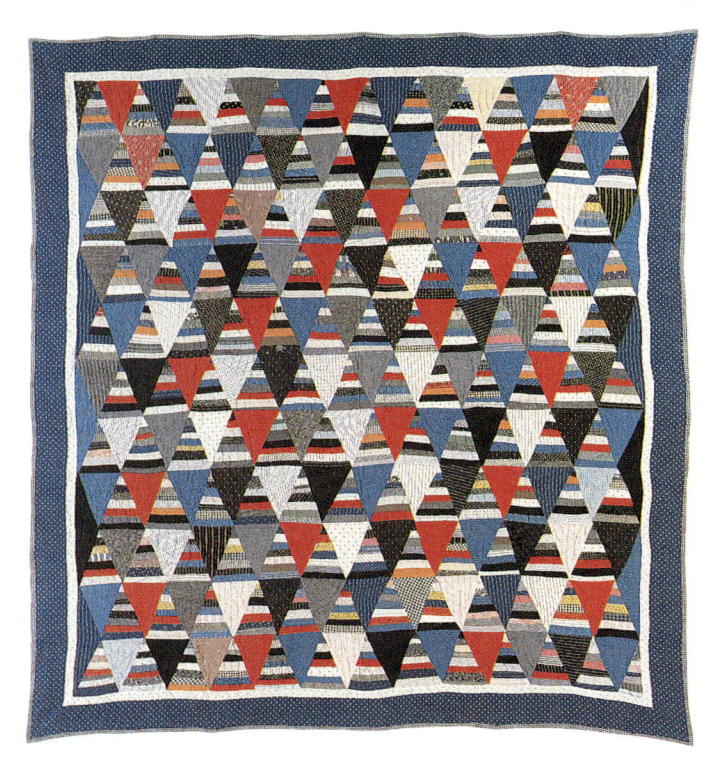

121. "Charm." 1900–1910. Pennsylvania. 81" x 74". The transition from nineteenth to twentieth century quilts can be seen in this fine example of a "Charm" quilt pieced with triangles of one large piece of fabric alternating with strip-pieced triangles. Photograph courtesy Bettie Mintz.

122. "Checkerboard Vortex." Ca. 1920. Probably New Jersey. 85" x 85". Extraordinarily contemporary in its design, this amazing quilt is a triumph of precise design and piecing, and it is an astonishing precursor of the art of Vasarely. (Collection of Oscar Appel)

123. "Broken Circles" or "Sunflowers." Ca. 1930. 85" x 89". Although a commercial offering—this pattern was published by the *Kansas City Star* in the 1930s—the maker's touch can be seen in the choice of the delightfully flashy colors of this vibrant quilt. (Collection of Sweet Nellie)

124. "Hexagonal Stars." Ca. 1935. 89" x 79". Like the best graphic quilts, this ice-cream-colored patchwork raises a question: Are these rows of morning-glory inspired flowers or a galaxy of six-pointed stars? Each of the colorful hexagons is made with pieced strips, giving the quilt extra detail and textural interest. (Private collection)

125. "Japanese Lanterns." Ca. 1925. 84" x 74". Like the jazz age, this quilt steps to a lively beat. Its kaleidoscope of colors keeps the eye dancing among it focal points: from the dark blue through the brightly colored strips joined by peach-colored stars and polka-dotted circles. Visual motion, rather than one or two recognizable images, is behind the success of this irresistible quilt. (Private collection)

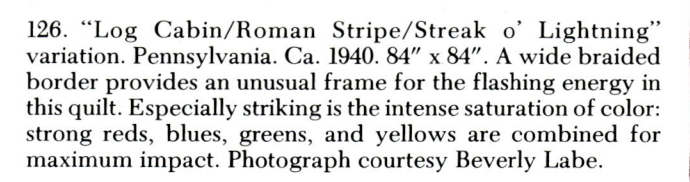

126. "Log Cabin/Roman Stripe/Streak o' Lightning" variation. Pennsylvania. Ca. 1940. 84" x 84". A wide braided border provides an unusual frame for the flashing energy in this quilt. Especially striking is the intense saturation of color: strong reds, blues, greens, and yellows are combined for maximum impact. Photograph courtesy Beverly Labe.

127. "Chief's Blanket." Ca. 1940. 84" x 82". Although the influence of Navajo weavings and colors is obvious here, this quilt also reflects elements of mainstream twentieth-century culture. Red, black, and gray, for example, were favorite choices for everything from Bakelite jewelry to cigarette lighters. Also, the triangular motifs in the border were typical of Art Deco design. (Collection of Rochelle Epstein)

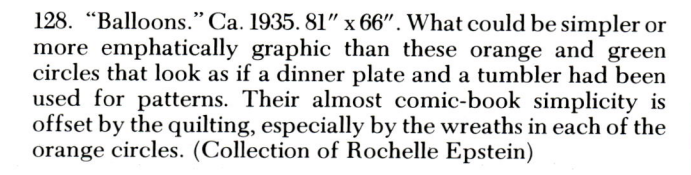

128. "Balloons." Ca. 1935. 81" x 66". What could be simpler or more emphatically graphic than these orange and green circles that look as if a dinner plate and a tumbler had been used for patterns. Their almost comic-book simplicity is offset by the quilting, especially by the wreaths in each of the orange circles. (Collection of Rochelle Epstein)

129. "Horn of Plenty." Ca. 1935. 95" x 76". There is "nothing more typical of our native America than this symbol of endless supply," said Stearns & Foster of their pattern #87. To make the design even more appealing, the company dredged up some allusions to the horn of plenty in Classical Greece. The municipal-office green in the quilt was a very popular color of the period. (Collection of Stearns & Foster)

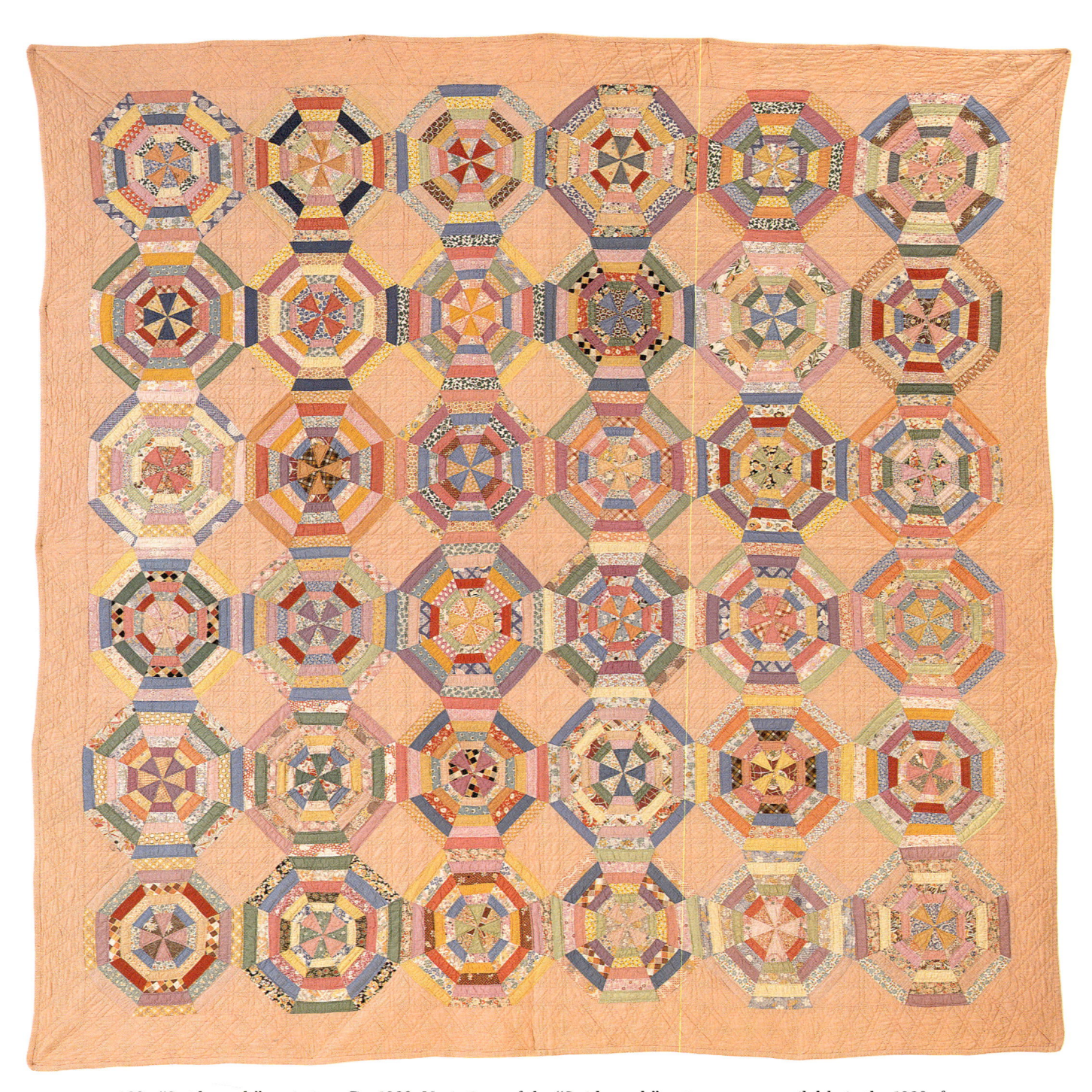

130. "Spiderweb" variation. Ca. 1930. Variations of the "Spiderweb" pattern were available in the 1930s from several sources, including Nancy Cabot's syndicated column written by Loretta Leitner Rising for the *Chicago Tribune*, and Grandma Dexter's pamphlets produced in Elgin, Illinois. The peach color of the background was very popular in the thirties. The bright color and kaleidoscopic form make this a joyous quilt. Photograph courtesy Kelter-Malcé Antiques.

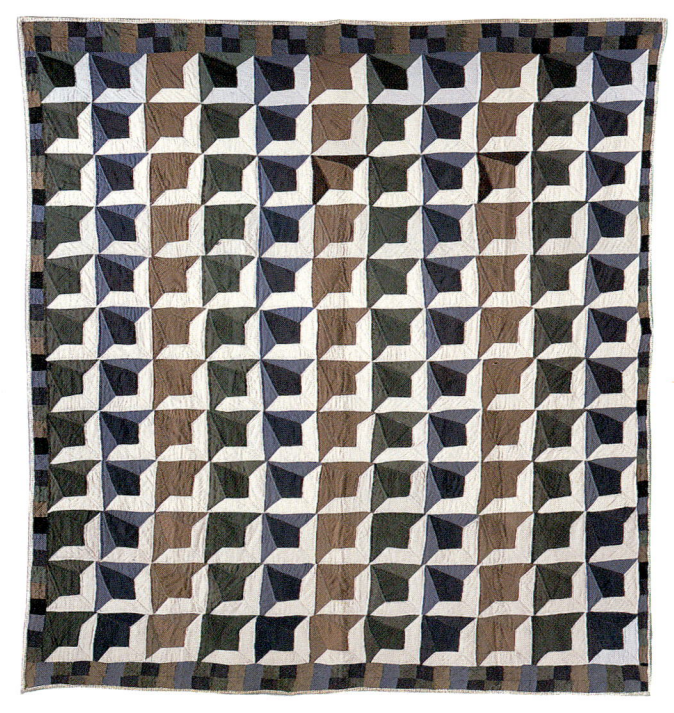

131. "Shadow Boxes." Ca. 1915. 83" x 74". Pennsylvania. The dramatic juxtaposition of light and shadow can be achieved in patchwork by using the humblest of materials guided by a keen eye for strong graphic design. (Private collection)

132. Log Cabin: "Light and Dark" and "Streak o' Lightning" combination. Ca. 1930. 78" x 76½". Although the "Log Cabin" style is one of the most important of the nineteenth century, this example clearly sparkles with a bright twentieth-century sensibility. Pieced with solids, less common in "Log Cabin" quilts, its peach and periwinkle blue create an upbeat Art Deco look, like the tiled floor of an ice cream parlor. (Collection of Gail and Jonathan Holstein)

133. "Chinese Coins." Midwestern Amish. Ca. 1935. 84" x 68". Relatively few examples of this pattern can be found, although it is a fairly simple one to execute. Midwestern Amish quiltmakers had their own ideas about choosing and arranging colors, and often used dark tones like blue and black for the backgrounds of their spreads, thus giving their quilts a distinctive and often fascinating style.

134. "Center Diamond." Ca. 1925. 84" x 75". Most Amish Diamonds were made in wool in Pennsylvania, particularly Lancaster County, between 1890 and 1910. This later version was rendered in brightly colored cottons, which midwestern Amish quiltmakers could purchase in their local fabric stores, often for making children's clothing. Photograph courtesy Laura Fisher.

# MY COUNTRY, TIS OF THEE

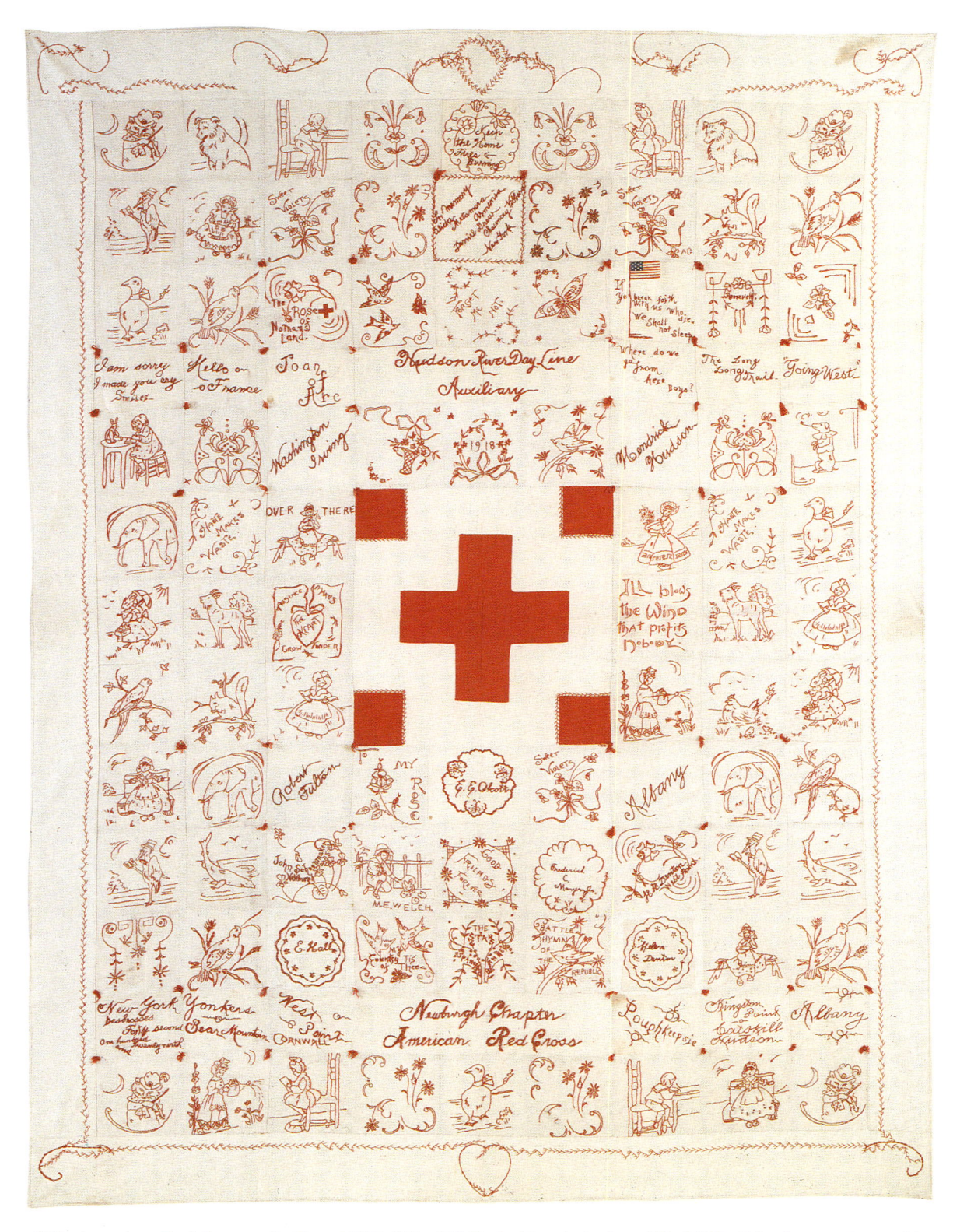

135. American Red Cross quilt. Dated 1918. 88" x 66". Probably stitched as a World War I fundraiser, this quilt's squares name various New York State Red Cross chapters, from Newburgh to Albany. Other patches bear whimsical illustrations—a dog smoking a pipe, for example—and pieties like "haste makes waste" and "keep the home fires burning." Poignant are the additional patches stitched as memorials to soldiers. (Private collection)

136. "Stars and Stripes." Dated 1917. 76" x 58". With patriotic fervor on the rise because of World War I, stars and stripes were a natural motif for quilters. With its graphic energy, this banner explodes with all the flag-waving, band-playing energy of a military parade. (Collection of Jo and Frank McClure)

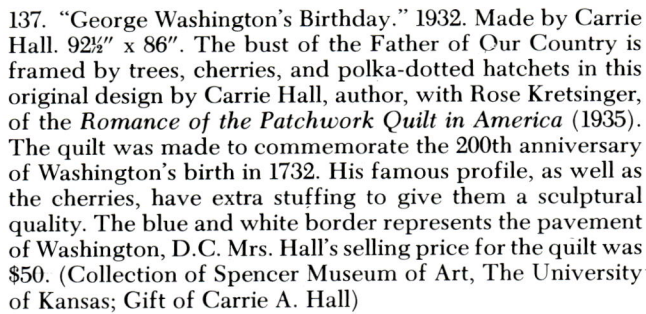

137. "George Washington's Birthday." 1932. Made by Carrie Hall. 92½" x 86". The bust of the Father of Our Country is framed by trees, cherries, and polka-dotted hatchets in this original design by Carrie Hall, author, with Rose Kretsinger, of the *Romance of the Patchwork Quilt in America* (1935). The quilt was made to commemorate the 200th anniversary of Washington's birth in 1732. His famous profile, as well as the cherries, have extra stuffing to give them a sculptural quality. The blue and white border represents the pavement of Washington, D.C. Mrs. Hall's selling price for the quilt was $50. (Collection of Spencer Museum of Art, The University of Kansas; Gift of Carrie A. Hall)

138. "Flag." 1932. Made by Mrs. Andy Hallford. Bangs, Texas. 72" x 79". Sent to President-elect Franklin Roosevelt in 1932, this quilt offers a thrifty as well as a patriotic salute. Mrs. Hallford made it from carefully saved red, white, and blue tobacco pouches. Her stars and stripes, set against a dynamic, rippling "Streak o' Lightning" background, actually seem to be waving in the breeze. An appliquéd and stuffed yellow flag pole makes a nice finishing touch. (Collection of the Franklin D. Roosevelt Library)

139, 140. "Donkey" and "Elephant." Leavenworth, Kansas. 1931, 1932. Made by Mrs. Jameson. The *Kansas City Star*, a popular pattern source for midwestern quilters, published these patterns: Giddap, the Donkey, and Ararat, the Elephant. Since the maker was a Democrat, it is said that she made Giddap slightly larger than Ararat, which she made for her Republican husband. Photographs courtesy Sandra Todaro.

141. "National Recovery Act." Dated 1933. Braymor, Missouri. The NRA Blue Eagle became one of the most famous and ubiquitous symbols of Depression America, for it was proudly displayed in the front windows of grocery stores and all sorts of other shops. This quilt surrounds the poster image with an energizing collection of stars and bars. Photograph courtesy Sandra Todaro.

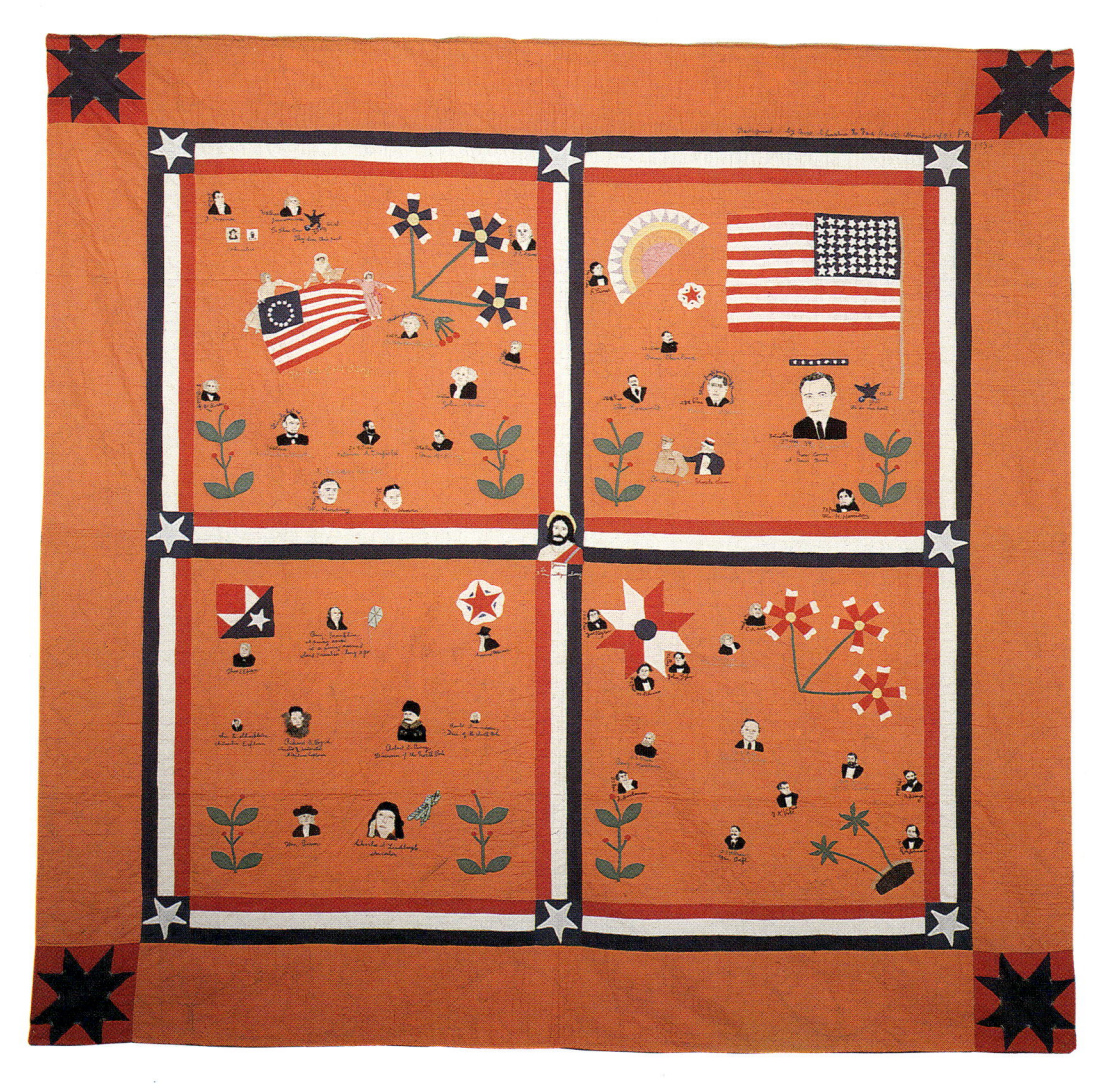

142. Commerorative appliqué. Dated 1934. Designed by Mrs. Charles G. Fox, Womelsdorf, Pennsylvania. 86" x 86". Set on Pennsylvania's favorite "punkin orange" background are a host of historical heroes with inscriptions: President Franklin D. Roosevelt; Admiral Perry; Conrad Weiser, a Lutheran pastor who was the leader of a German group that settled in the area; Arctic explorer Ernest Shackleton; William Penn; Charles A. Lindbergh; Robert E. Peary, discoverer of the North Pole; Thomas Edison; Betsy Ross; Uncle Sam; and a quote by Ben Franklin: "A penny saved is a penny earned." Quilters occasionally reversed the American flag, as seen here. (Collection of Susan and David Cunningham)

143. "FDR's Election." 1936. 84" x 75". In honor of FDR's landslide victory against Al Landon, this quilt features the Democrat's donkey. Stars are embroidered with each state's allotted electoral votes. Roosevelt received 523, as noted by the figure in the center of the quilt. Landon garnered eight. His total is recorded in the bottom center square, above the stars of the two wayward states he carried, Maine and Vermont. (Collection of the Franklin D. Roosevelt Library)

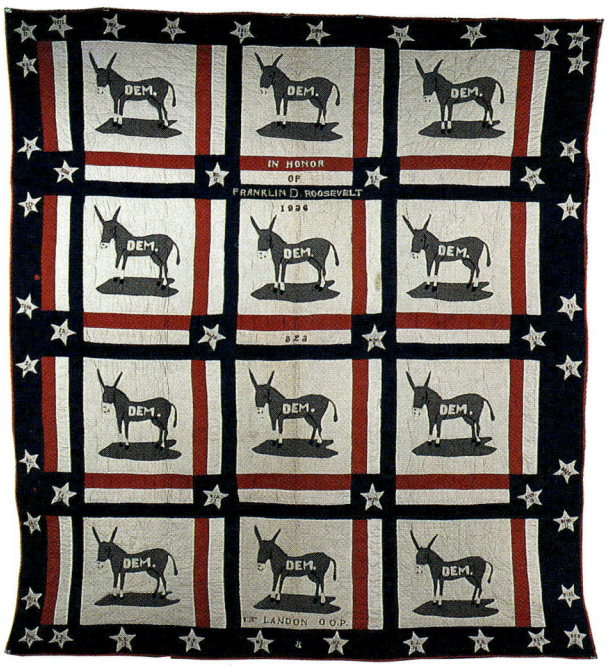

144. "Historic U.S.A." 1936. Texas. 95" x 75". Made by Fanny and Charles Normann. Thirty-one presidents surround a textile picture of the signing of the Declaration of Independence in this piece commissioned by the late husband of Artie Fultz Davis of Navasota, Texas. Washington tops the oval of portraits, with Roosevelt and Lincoln featured, along with favorite American symbols: eagles, flags, Liberty Bells, and the Statue of Liberty. (Courtesy Mrs. Artie Fultz Davis and Star of the Republic Museum, Washington, Texas)

145. "Eleanor Roosevelt Album." 1940. Satin. Made by Callie Jeffress Fanning Smith. Sulfur Springs, Texas. 77½" x 61". The embroidered words "to our First Lady," were meant literally here. Sent as a gift to Mrs. Roosevelt in March 1940, the quilt's squares portray the First Lady at various periods in her life from childhood to the White House. In each scene, Mrs. Roosevelt is dressed in intricately appliquéd fashions, complete with realistic trimmings, and her face is masterfully painted on fabric. (Collection of the Franklin D. Roosevelt Library)

146. "Stars and Stripes." Ca. 1940. 80" x 90". Had Betsy Ross designed a quilt instead of a flag, she may well have positioned her field of blue in the center, as this quilter did, so that it could star on a bed. She might also have opted for six-pointed stars, which, although they take up more space, are easier to piece than those with five points. (Collection of Elizabeth and Richard Kramer)

147. "Century of Progress." 1933. Made by Mrs. W. B. Lathouse, Warren, Ohio. 82" x 66". The Century of Progress Exposition inspired quilters across the nation to dig into our history for subjects relating to patriotism and progress. Pictured are Franklin Delano Roosevelt (unfinished) under the caption "Hope of a Nation," George Washington, "Father of Our Country," and Abraham Lincoln, "The Emancipator." Transportation is highlighted with an appliqué *Mayflower*, the airship *Macon*, a bicycle, train, balloon, and an automobile. Modern appliances, such as a washing machine and a vacuum cleaner, illustrate how things have progressed from the simple, country life depicted at the bottom of the central panel. Photograph courtesy America Hurrah Antiques. (Private collection)

104

148. "Victory Is Our Goal." 1945. Made by Mrs. W. B. Lathouse, Warren, Ohio. 88" x 76". Bursts of patriotism can be effectively expressed in quilts; this example was made by a quilter with professional experience who came to America from Wales in 1922. Pictured here are Roosevelt, MacArthur, Stalin, Churchill; flags of Britain, Russia, Australia, and China; and the Morse code's three-dots-and-a-dash symbolizing V for victory. Photograph courtesy America Hurrah Antiques. (Private collection)

# GOING TO PIECES

149. "Sawtooth" variation. Ca. 1910. 73" x 73". At the center of each of the large squares are sixteen-patch blocks. The fabrics are from the turn of the century. A good example of the emphasis on frugality that persisted into the twentieth century, the quilt was apparently made from the scraps on hand. Many of its long rows, intended to be one single color, had to be supplemented with scraps of different prints. Photograph courtesy Noreen Lewandowski.

150. "Clamshells." Ca. 1910. 92" x 72". Several pattern sources offered variations of this pattern, including Grandmother Clark, Ladies· Art Catalog Co., and Old Chelsea Station Needlecraft Service. As this sampler of pre-World War I fabrics shows, the fairly reserved color palette reminds one of the tiny plaids and checks of earlier homespuns. It was after the war in the carefree twenties that we find an explosion of bright pastels. This quilt is simple in its pattern, yet highly evocative. Densely ordered, the clamshells almost appear to represent a sea of faces, the crowded melting pot one would see in city streets, filled with immigrants from many shores.

151. "Parrots." Ca. 1900. Birdsboro, Lancaster County, Pennsylvania. The feathering in this portrayal of exotic birds and the airy detail in the tree and urn with flowers are made with a vast mosaic of pieces—7920 in all. This total may seem astonishingly high until one looks closely and realizes that the red-dotted white background is also a pieced mosaic. The whole painting in fabric is handsomely framed with a classic chain border. Photograph courtesy M. Finkel & Daughter.

152. "Irish Chain." Ca. 1935. "Could this be the quilt you've been saving all those scrap-bag pieces for?" queried *Capper's Weekly* in Topeka, Kansas, which first published the pattern for this Irish Chain variation in January 1934 under the name, "The Rainbow Around the World." Dynamic by design, this quilt is even more striking because of the high contrast between the peach blocks and their green and black pieced frames. All three colors were highly fashionable in the thirties. Photograph courtesy Kelter-Malcé Antiques.

153. "Grandmother's Flower Garden" variation. Ca. 1930. 82" x 84". Here is a highly unusual variation on one of America's favorite patterns that is more commonly executed in pale, sentimental colors. The use of a dramatic, dark background, on which are sewn single rows of patches linking small clusters of flowers to the main garden, and with a picket fence on two borders, make this an appealing composition, suggesting the form of a butterfly overall. Photograph courtesy Wild Goose Chase Quilt Gallery. (Collection of Gary Brockman)

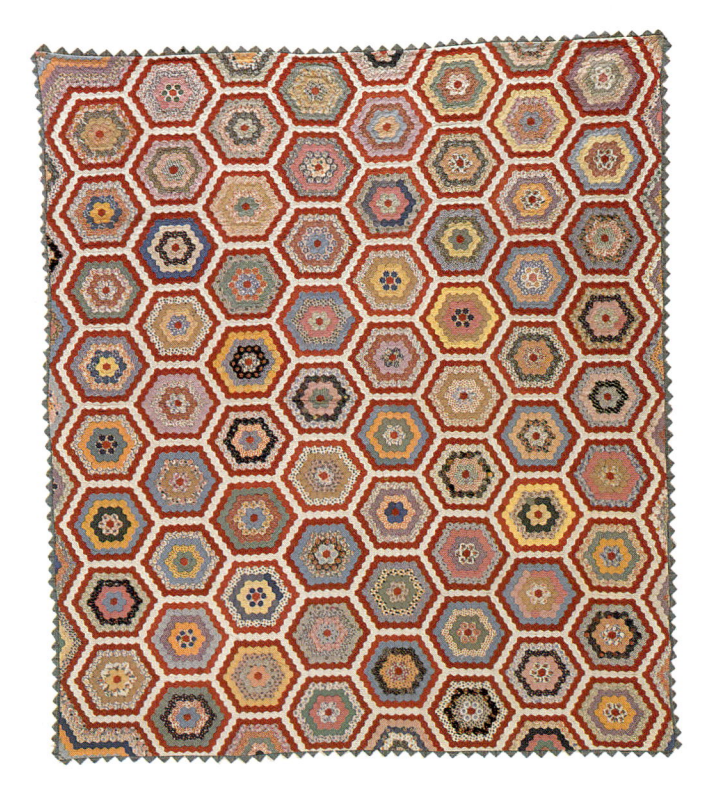

154. "Grandmother's Flower Garden" variation. Ca. 1940. Midwestern U.S.A. 78" x 64". Variations of colorful flower gardens made of tiny hexagons were among the three most popular patterns of the twentieth century. The major pattern sources, such as Stearns & Foster, all offered versions, sometimes calling it "Garden Walk" or "Martha Washington's Flower Garden," as did *Capper's Weekly*. This relatively late example is differentiated by its spicy red and white frames for the hexagons. The snappy color combinations give pep to the geometry of the pattern, creating an energetic mosaic, rather than the usual, more sentimental profusion of paler hues. Photograph courtesy Judy Corman.

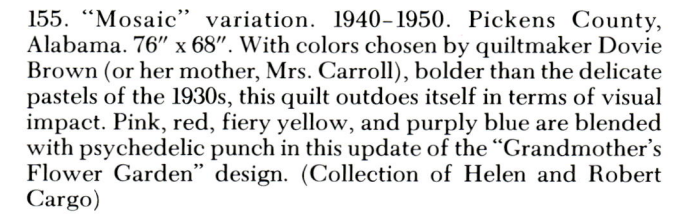

155. "Mosaic" variation. 1940-1950. Pickens County, Alabama. 76" x 68". With colors chosen by quiltmaker Dovie Brown (or her mother, Mrs. Carroll), bolder than the delicate pastels of the 1930s, this quilt outdoes itself in terms of visual impact. Pink, red, fiery yellow, and purply blue are blended with psychedelic punch in this update of the "Grandmother's Flower Garden" design. (Collection of Helen and Robert Cargo)

156. "Hexagonal Mosaic." Ca. 1940. More than a century before this quilt was made, English quilters were piecing "Mosaic" or "Honeycomb" spreads, cutting and sewing together hundreds of hexagons from beautiful printed chintz, often in soft, elegant hues. Here is a dramatic contrast in style, the maker having chosen to approach the pattern in a bold, brash, and startlingly modern manner, using strong, uninhibited colors in a carefully controlled, intriguing composition. (Collection of Laurie Schwarm)

157. "Miniaturized Postage Stamp" variation. 1939. Made by Mrs. B. W. Riley, Farson, Iowa. 104" x 81". The statistics are staggering on this piecework extravaganza, which captured first prize at the Eldon, Iowa, fair in 1940. 69,649 pieces and 1,087 hours went into its creation. A total of 3,694 yards of thread were required for the sewing, and Mrs. Riley estimated the number of stitches at 1,810,874. Weight is not generally considered a vital statistic for quilts, but this one, weighing in at 7½ pounds, deserves mentioning. Figuring on the basis of an eight-hour day, it took Mrs. Riley 194 days, not counting the 425 hours it took to cut the pieces of cloth—or lunch breaks! This is one of about 200 quilts made by Mrs. Riley, who was also accomplished at embroidery, crocheting, and knitting. (Collection of Donna and Bryce Hamilton)

158. Mrs. B. W. Riley, Farson, Iowa. 1940. Looking none the worse for wear, considering the monumental achievement hanging behind her (fig. 157), Mrs. Riley's place among the remarkable quiltmakers of the twentieth century seems assured. Photograph courtesy Donna and Bryce Hamilton.

159. "Broken Dishes." 1940–1950. Tuscaloosa, Alabama. 84" x 70". Despite the close, painstaking work it took to piece each of the 10,752 patches in this tour-de-force, its maker had an instinctive feeling for the overall effect of her color choices. Her carefully color-themed squares come together to make a remarkable whole, a composition equally striking when viewed from afar. (Collection of Helen and Robert Cargo)

160. "Snail's Trail" or "Labyrinth." Ca. 1935. 76" x 70". The creator of this piece may have been inspired by printed fabrics of a century earlier. By enlarging the blue snaky design and letting it wander through a crazy patchwork of 1930s scraps, a brand new "modern" effect was achieved. Photograph courtesy Laura Fisher.

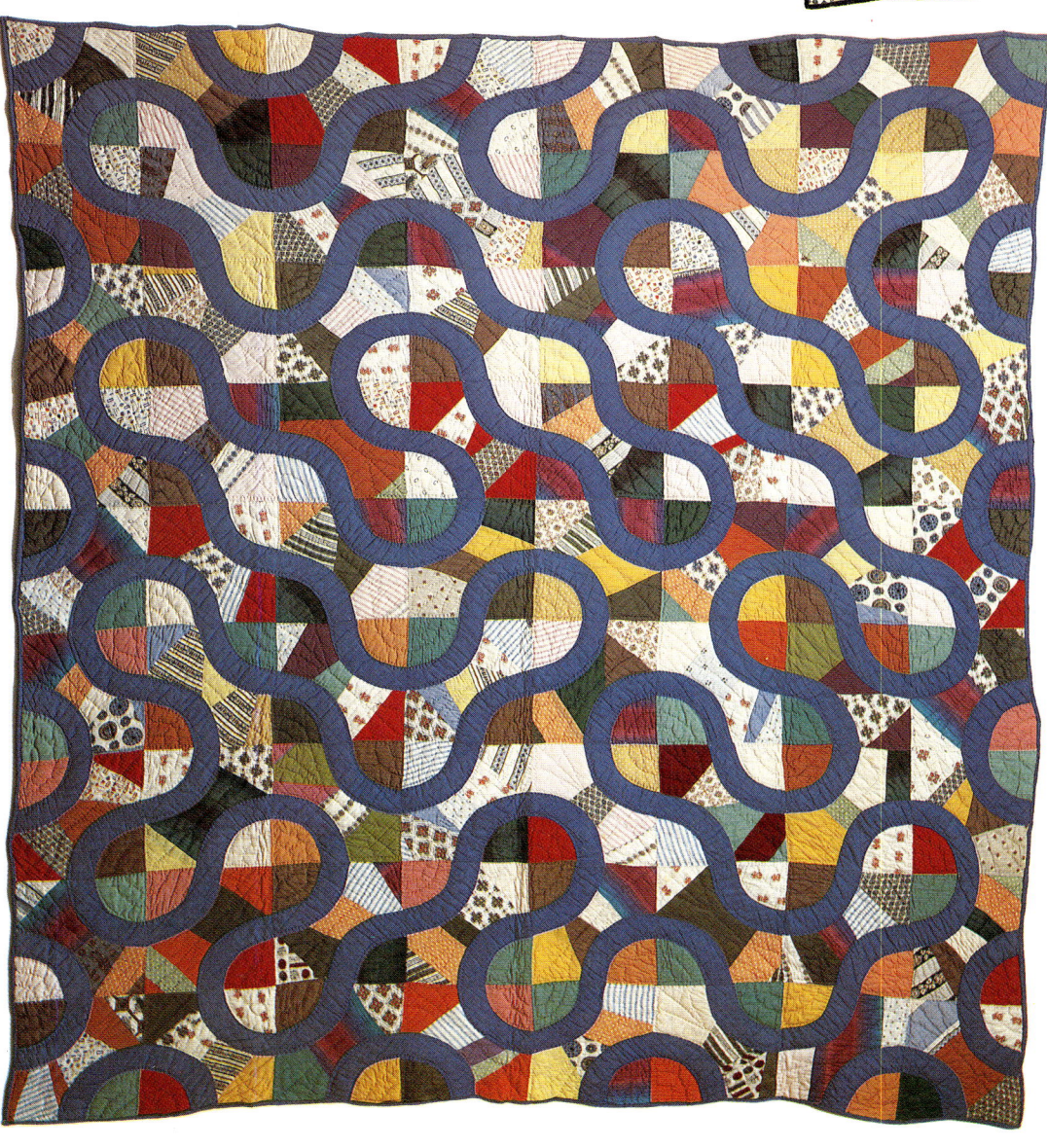

161. "Mosaic." Made by Grace McCance Snyder. Ca. 1940. North Platte, Nebraska. 99" x 100". English-born Albert Small of Ottawa, Illinois, executed this design in 1939 in a quilt using 63,460 hexagonal pieces. Mrs. Snyder, working from a small black and white photograph, reproduced the pattern in her own dazzling array of stained-glass colors. While she did not top his record number of pieces with this quilt, she did surpass it in 1943 with her "Flower Basket Petit Point" (fig. 162). In true *Guinness-Book-of-Records* style, however, Mr. Small was reported in 1939 to have nearly completed a spread with 123,000 pieces. (See *Historic Quilts* by Florence Peto, p. 128). Regardless of who wears the most-pieces-in-patchwork crown, Mrs. Synder's prominence in twentieth-century quilting remains unsurpassed. Photograph courtesy Nellie Snyder Yost. (Collection of Billie Thornburg)

162. "Flower Basket Petit Point." 1943. Made by Grace McCance Snyder. North Platte, Nebraska, 94" x 93". Adapted from a design on a china plate, this textile candy-box confection was created by skillfully piecing 87,789 tiny triangles. Its maker, determined to set a record for the highest number of pieces in a quilt, produced one of the most impressive and charming patchworks of the twentieth century. (Collection of Nellie Snyder Yost)

# ONE PICTURE IS WORTH 1,000 WORDS

163. "The Homestead." Early twentieth century. Signed F. Cochran. 72" x 92". Naive American paintings have become recognized in recent years as a highly valuable part of our heritage. *Textile* paintings, such as this extraordinary example, by home artists working with whatever materials were available, including the use here of ordinary cellophane for window glass, are extremely rare. The attention to detail is wonderful, and it records a rural scene as viewed by an inspired, nonacademic American artist. Photograph courtesy of Sotheby's. (Private collection)

164. "Pictograph." Ca. 1900. Crow Creek Reservation, South Dakota. 78" x 70". Made by a Sioux Indian as a gift of friendship for a South Dakota homesteader, this piece resembles the painted deer and buffalo hides created by American Indians. Here is a brilliant group of images: hunting scenes, peace pipes with tomahawks, tribal dances, and even beavers that look like kangaroos. (Collection of David Schorsch)

165. "The Beautiful Unequaled Gardens of Eden and Elenale." Hawaii. Early twentieth century, before 1918. 78½" x 92". In addition to patriotic quilts, Hawaiian quiltmakers, taught by missionary wives in the 1830s, were fond of story-telling quilts. Here, two stories are told: the banishment of Adam and Eve from the Garden of Eden, and a portrayal of Elenale and Leinaala, two royal figures in Hawaiian history. Although it is not presently known who made the quilt, recent information indicates the maker was a Hawaiian man. (Collection of Honolulu Academy of Arts)

166. "American Life." Made by Mrs. Cecil White. Ca. 1925. Hartford, Connecticut. 77" x 66". Textile folk art at its most delightful is captured in this "album" of scenes from everyday life. Among the vignettes are a wedding, a mouse scare, ethnic groups, farm chores, sports and, in the borders, modes of transportation—all created here by a very perceptive and warmly expressive artist. Photograph courtesy America Hurrah Antiques. (Private collection)

167. "Mountain Dreams." 1920–1930. Found in upper New York State. Mountains loom in the background of this picturesque view of life in a log cabin, conveying a dreamlike quality of getting-away-from-it-all. Despite the extreme care and skill that went into creating this fabric painting, the maker did not feel it was important to sign or date the work, and, so, she (or he) remains anonymous. (Courtesy Shelburne Museum)

168. "Settling of the West." Started March 1931; completed September 1932. Made by Mildred Jacob Chappell. 103" x 83". Conestoga wagons wend their way from East to West across the center of this prize-winning quilt, which bears an embroidered salute "to the Pioneer," as "indomitable" and "unafraid." Scenes around the border, also labeled and punctuated by poems, depict Lewis and Clark, Geronimo, the Pony Express, and other legends of the West. In a letter, Mrs. Chappell declared she made this quilt "as a labor of love" for history, regretting only that she had not lived one hundred years earlier to experience these "stirring times." A paper label, ribbons, and a metal pin, reminders of the quilt's success at contests such as the Century of Progress national competition, remain attached to the back of the piece. (Collection of Pat and Rich Gartheoffner)

169. "Mennonite Picnic." Ca. 1930. Pennsylvania. 82" x 84". Although surrounded by an unlikely parade of fashionable women, who perhaps stepped out of a commercial pattern, this quilt is actually an enchanting depiction of a Mennonite community picnic. At its center is a table whose cloth is untacked on the sides, as are the aprons of the two women who preside over it. Sailboats on the horizon symbolize the maker's ancestors arriving in America. Graves in the churchyard are marked with initials. A powerful narrative, this textile painting captures a special day in the life of rural Pennsylvania's past. (Collection of Nancy and Sam Starr)

170. "The Matterhorn." 1934. Colorado. Made by Myrtle Mae Fortner. 102" x 84". Inspired by a niece's trip to Switzerland, this textile picture of a colorfully shaded mountain, rocks, cabins, and a stream is made of 9,153 one-inch squares. Mrs. Fortner (1880–1956), in addition to being a quilter, was a rug maker, stamp collector, oil painter, and poet. One poem, "Reward," stated: "I quilt/With stitches small/and know, a century hence/Posterity will gasp and say/'How neat.'" Indeed, her words ring true as "The Matterhorn" is now part of The Denver Art Museum collection. Photograph courtesy The Denver Art Museum.

171. "Peace with the Indians." 1938. Ohio. Inscribed 1788–1938. 79" x 91". Creating paintings with appliquéd cloth presents one of the most difficult challenges to a quilter. Choosing a worthy subject, designing the picture, making the patterns, selecting the colors, cutting the pieces, sewing them on, quilting the piece, finishing the edges—all of the difficult tasks involved constitute a formidable undertaking at which only the most accomplished needleworkers succeed. Commemorating the treaty made with the Indians on the banks of the Marietta River, Ohio, this fabric painting is an outstanding example of the quilter as a folk artist. (Private collection)

172. "Covered Bridge." 1940–1950. 71" x 64". An appreciative couple surveys this pastoral scene with its covered bridge and oddly spired church. Apparently, they have just stepped into the quilted picture, for the woman's billowing skirt still dangles over the frame. Photograph courtesy Kathy and Frank Gaglio.

173. "Ninety and Nine." Made by Emma Andres. 1947. 60" x 48". Prescott, Arizona. An avid newspaper reader, Miss Andres became a long-distance admirer of Charles Pratt, a quilter in Philadelphia about whom a number of newspaper articles were published. After becoming pen-pals with Mr. Pratt, she made a replica of his "Ninety and Nine" quilt that shows Jesus carrying a lamb on His shoulders. Miss Andres used half-inch squares—the original was made with three-quarter-inch squares—and she spent five years dying and sewing the tiny pieces. Photograph courtesy Laurene Sinema.

174. "Quilt Show." Made by Bertha Stenge. Illinois. 1943. 93" x 78". Thirteen favorite patterns are displayed in miniature—each approximately a six-inch square—by attractive, appliquéd ladies in this prize-winning, original design. Fifty-two different pieced blocks are reproduced in the border. This delightful quilt show would be an important visual aid in any course on quilting in America. Photograph courtesy Joyce Gross. (Collection of Frances Stenge Traynor)

175. "The Quilting Bee." Pieced and appliquéd by Bertha Stenge. Ca. 1948. Illinois. 81" x 77". The center of this framed medallion quilt is an appliqué reproduction of a painting created by an unknown Virginia artist around 1854. The multiple borders of piecework are reminiscent of earlier English quilts. The Art Institute of Chicago recognized Mrs. Stenge's talents, as well as the importance of quilts in America, before this quilt was made, having honored her in 1943 with a one-woman show. Mrs. Stenge's beautiful work is among the most respected and admired of twentieth-century quiltmakers. Photograph courtesy Joyce Gross. (Collection of Frances Stenge Traynor)

# CHANGING THE SUBJECT

176. "Album." Made by Pocahontas Virginia Gay. Fluvanna County, Virginia. Ca. 1900. 67½" x 67½". Wool. A descendant of Pocahontas, this quilt's maker has presented an impressive "slide show" of subject matter important in her life, including a figure representing her famous ancestor, a number of animals and birds, a memorial to T.V. Gay, and portraits inscribed Davis, Andrew Jackson, and Lee. One block illustrates a child and dog, one asking the other, "Can you talk?" Photograph courtesy the Smithsonian Institution.

177. "Sampler." Ca. 1910. 70" x 47". A dazzling array of patterns is showcased here, including Le Moyne Star, Log Cabin, Cross, and Broken Dishes. The primitive style of this pieced quilt suggests it could have been a learning piece made by a young girl. (Collection of Annette and George Amann)

178. "Map of New York State." Ca. 1910. New York. 72" x 70". It is obvious that the maker of this "Crazy" quilt textile map did not live in eastern Long Island, for only half the island (at the bottom right corner) is shown on the quilt. Each county, such as "Dutchess" and "Ulster," is labeled with its initial. The result is a colorful and most unusual "Crazy" quilt. (Private collection)

179. "Leaves" quilt top. 1923. Kansas. 92" x 84". One hundred twenty-two different leaves in various shades of green are delicately appliquéd here on a plain white background, and the result is a botanist's delight. (Collection of Spencer Museum of Art, The University of Kansas)

180. "Fauna and Flora." Made by Mittie Barrier. Dated·1920. Silk, cotton, wool. 80″ x 70″. Although the elaborately decorative Victorian "Crazy" quilt reached its popularity before the end of the nineteenth century, a number of quilts of this type were made through the first quarter of the twentieth century. This needlework "album" contains a whole menagerie: ducks, geese, horses, rabbits, squirrels—even two crocodiles! (Collection of Cathy Shoe)

181. "Cherry Tree." 1936. Made by Charlotte Jane Whitehill. 84" x 82". Cherry Trees and Robins, an appliqué quilt from 1820, was the inspiration for this cheerful and expert piece of needlework. (Collection of The Denver Art Museum)

182. "The Peacock." Ca. 1932. Appliqué. Made by Hannah Haynes Headlee. Topeka, Kansas. 95" x 75". Hannah Haynes Headlee (1866–1943) was always considered the artist in her family, making ends meet by teaching china painting and watercolor. When she took up quilting in the late 1920s, she drew on her art background and incorporated sophisticated Art Nouveau motifs such as this peacock into her quilting. Note how the flowers in the border repeat the color and design of the peacock's plumes. Photograph courtesy Marie Shirer.

183. "The Cranes." Ca. 1934. Appliqué. Made by Hannah Haynes Headlee. Topeka, Kansas. 93" x 72". A major influence on Hannah Haynes Headlee's quilts was her niece, artist Pauline Shirer. Their association began when Mrs. Headlee gave Pauline art lessons on the front porch. Mrs. Headlee was not allowed inside the house because, having been married three times by 1910, she was considered somewhat scandalous. However, by 1914, Pauline's family changed their minds and allowed Mrs. Headlee to chaperone Pauline in New York, where she had been accepted at art school. "The Cranes," probably the most beautifully designed of Mrs. Headlee's quilts, contains details contributed by Pauline, such as the butterfly and the swirling water, which can also be found in her paintings of around 1932. Photograph courtesy Marie Shirer.

184. "Astrology." Ca. 1935. 108" x 87". Any guest who slept under this quilt was treated to a thumbnail character analysis: "spiritual, intuitive, agreeable, and romantic" was embroidered around the sign of Pisces, for example. Although it is natural for the twelve signs of the zodiac to be set in a galaxy of stars, the use of red, white, and blue gives the quilt an extra, flaglike impact. Offered under the name "Old Almanac Quilt," this pattern was a series quilt, meaning that it was offered one block at a time by newspapers from October 1932 to January 1933. Nancy Page, a pseudonym for designer Florence LaGanke, was credited as being the creator of this quilt. Photograph courtesy Stella Rubin. (Collection of Jane Braddock)

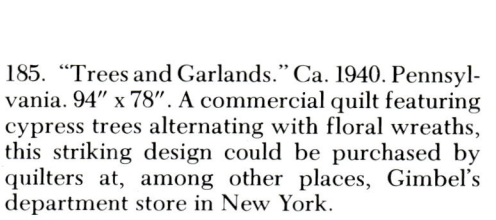

185. "Trees and Garlands." Ca. 1940. Pennsylvania. 94" x 78". A commercial quilt featuring cypress trees alternating with floral wreaths, this striking design could be purchased by quilters at, among other places, Gimbel's department store in New York.

# FOR CHILDREN OF ALL AGES

186. "Funny Papers." Made by the four children of Augustine and Jane Savery. 1916. Middlefield, Massachusetts. 90" x 74". Mutt and Jeff and their funny-papers cohorts appear to have been the inspiration for this amusing collection of figures, created as a family project during the winter of 1916. Little Orphan Annie is missing as she did not make her debut until 1924. (Private collection)

187. "Alphabet." Dated 1930. 36" x 24". Nancy Page, from Publishers Syndicate, New York, offered the pattern for one block of this quilt each week in newspapers. However, if one missed getting the paper one week, the pattern was also available by mail order. By around 1936, the pattern was offered in kit form by Mary McElwain of Walworth, Wisconsin. Presumably, the last block in this jolly children's piece did not allow space to illustrate a xylophone, a yellowbird, and a zebra; thus, an affectionate "You" was substituted with the suggestion that the name of the quilt's recipient be added. (Private collection)

188. "Sunbonnet Sue." Ca. 1930. 65" x 44". Twentieth-century quilters had a fondness for this sweet character, which resulted in frequent nation-wide appearances, at time flirting with over-exposure. Here, however, she is pleasingly portrayed in a wardrobe of fifteen period dresses with nicely coordinated balloon accessories. Photograph courtesy Laura Fisher.

189. "Menagerie." Ca. 1930. 102" x 80". Appliquéd animals, ranging from ambling elephants to barnyard hens, are given fully illustrated settings in this narrative quilt. The large size of this animal-kingdom quilt allows each creature to be seen in triplicate. (Private collection)

190. "Swan and Deer." Ca. 1930. 82" x 71½". A swan, swimming in a pond, is at the center of a pastoral landscape that does not ignore the modern. Electric wires span the horizon and a plane flies overhead. A young duckling, seemingly floating in heaven in a tiny pond of its own, has been added to cover the child's pillow. (Private collection)

191. "The Elephant's Child." Ca. 1934. This is a delightful example of the art of telling stories for children with textiles. The story is "How the Elephant Got Its Trunk" from Rudyard Kipling's *Just So Stories*. The designer of this kit quilt #2895 was E. Buckner Kirk, and the kit, which was offered for $5.00 by *Woman's Home Companion* in February 1934, contained stamped muslin, calico appliqué pieces, embroidery floss, and directions. The calico pieces were treated with a special process so that they would not require turning under and yet would not fray. Photograph courtesy Stella Rubin.

192. "Nursery Rhyme." Ca. 1930. 52" x 35". Although the doormat reads "Welcome," anyone who knows about the old woman who lived in a shoe realizes that guests would present a crisis situation. In this commercially produced scene, however, she and all her children—save two teary-eyed tots—seem cheerfully content with their foothold on life. Aunt Martha Studios of Kansas City, Missouri, produced patterns with appeal to children. (Private collection)

193. "Bambi." Ca. 1930. This peaceful country scene showing a family of deer at rest recalls fond childhood memories of Bambi. The top section of this quilt was designed for tucking over a pillow at the head of the bed. Photograph courtesy Stella Rubin.

194. "Casper the Ghost." Ca. 1945. 56½" x 39". A visit to the seashore, a ride down a rainbow, and clean-up time are some of the adventures of Casper, the Friendly Ghost, illustrated and captured in this quilt. Casper, the hero of television cartoons beginning in 1963, first gained stardom in the 1940s when Paramount cast him in theatrical cartoons. (Collection of Heather MacCrae)

132

# FLIGHTS OF FANCY

195. Embroidered picture, probably English. 1910–1920. 24½" x 23". Showing what English needleworkers were creating in the early twentieth century, Little Bo Beep, wearing an appliquéd dress and weeping embroidered tears, mourns the loss of her sheep in an elaborate pastoral scene. Bo Peep and other nursery-rhyme figures were a popular source of inspiration for quilts and needlework of all types. (Collection of Mariette Gomez)

196. Detail from an embroidered quilt. 1890–1910. This well-fed group of cats, both cool and affectionate in nature, was embroidered using a transfer pattern. Their whiskered grins and generously proportioned shapes are executed in red on white turkey work, a popular embroidery named after the red threads in Turkish carpets. (Private collection)

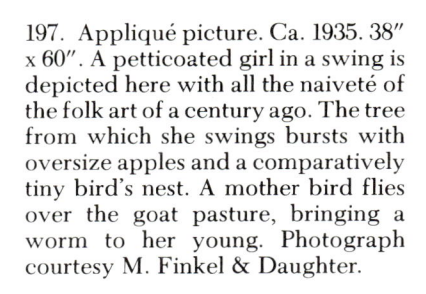

197. Appliqué picture. Ca. 1935. 38" x 60". A petticoated girl in a swing is depicted here with all the naiveté of the folk art of a century ago. The tree from which she swings bursts with oversize apples and a comparatively tiny bird's nest. A mother bird flies over the goat pasture, bringing a worm to her young. Photograph courtesy M. Finkel & Daughter.

133

198. "Pictorial Yo-yo." Ca. 1925. Tiny, bottle-cap-like circles of fabric offer a unique collage of images, including mother ducks, their wings marked in yellow, leading parades of floating ducklings around three sides. A yellow-breasted bird perches on an enormous rose that dwarfs the basket of flowers at its left. Peeking between the circles is a pink lining that provides additional color depth. Rather like a pointillist painting, this is a quilt whose images might best be viewed from a distance. Photograph courtesy Kelter-Malcé Antiques.

199. "Tennis Lady." 17" x 17".   200. "Lady with Butterfly." 15" x 15".   201. "Motoring Lady." 17½" x 17½".

Stamped and pretinted pillow kits. For the needleworker who fancied herself the glamour girl, these kits, which simply needed to be embroidered, left her plenty of time for gardening, tennis, and driving, the latter of which evidently could be accomplished without keeping one's eyes on the road. The JBK Company offered unfinished pillow backs, such as the #596 Sport Pillow, for the sophisticated needleworker "on-the-go."

202. Pillow prestamped and embroidered with a Spanish galleon. Ca. 1925. 16¼" x 25". See figure 203, page 136. (Private collection)

135

203. *Spanish Galleon* by Lee Mero. Ca. 1925. 6″ x 4½″. During the 1920s the motif of the sailing ship enjoyed great popularity as the symbol par excellence of the romantic atmosphere and charm that the shelter magazines of the period said should characterize the homes of their readers. Considering the pervasiveness of the sailing-ship motif in the decorative arts, the authors have been puzzled by never having seen it used on a quilt of the period. (Private collection)

204. "Tea Cozy/Toaster Cover." Pieced felt. Ca. 1930. 10" x 14". The Art Deco streamlining of this machine-stitched cover matches the "Moderne" look that was smartening up home appliances. However, its zippy shape is tempered with a suitably down home touch—flowers with cut-felt centers that seem to have been borrowed from a churchgoer's hat. (Private collection)

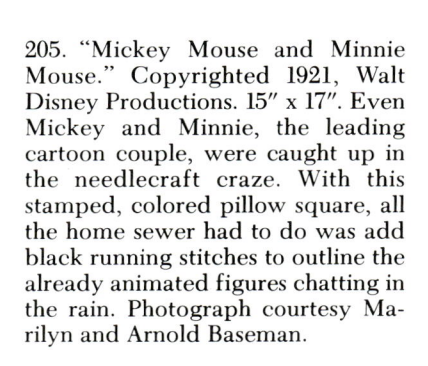

205. "Mickey Mouse and Minnie Mouse." Copyrighted 1921, Walt Disney Productions. 15" x 17". Even Mickey and Minnie, the leading cartoon couple, were caught up in the needlecraft craze. With this stamped, colored pillow square, all the home sewer had to do was add black running stitches to outline the already animated figures chatting in the rain. Photograph courtesy Marilyn and Arnold Baseman.

# BIBLIOGRAPHY

Almy, Patricia, ed. *Nimble Treasures*. Sapulpa, Okla.: 1969–1975.

*American Home Magazine*. November 1937.

*Arts & Crafts: A Bibliography for Craftsmen*. Washington, D.C.: National Gallery of Art, Smithsonian Institution, 1949.

Bacon, Lenice Ingram. *American Patchwork Quilts*. New York: William Morrow, 1973.

Bentley (no first name given). *Beautifying the Suburban Home or Bungalow*. Pamphlet. Artamo Embroidery Company, 1915.

Beyer, Alice. *Quilting*. Chicago: Leisure Hobby Series, 1934.

Brackman, Barbara. *An Encyclopedia of Pieced Patterns*. vol. 1–8. Lawrence, Kans.: Prairie Flower Publications, 1983.

———. "Midwestern Pattern Sources." *Uncoverings 19890*. Mill Valley, Calif.: The American Quilt Study Group, 1980.

Brody, Jane E. "Personal Health." *The New York Times*, April 6, 1985.

Carlisle, Lilian Baker. *Quilts at the Shelburne Museum*. Shelburne, Vt.: Shelburne Museum Publication, 1957.

Clements, John. *Chronology of the United States*. New York: McGraw-Hill, 1975.

Colby, Averil. *Patchwork*. London: B.T. Batsford, 1958.

———. *Patchwork Quilts*. New York: Charles Scribner's Sons, 1965.

Cooper, Patricia, and Buferd, Norma Bradley. *The Quilters: Women and Domestic Arts*. New York: Doubleday, 1977.

Danner, Scioto Imhoff. "Memoirs." Unpublished manuscript. El Dorado, Kansas, July 22, 1970.

———. *Mrs. Danner's Fifth Quilt Book*. Published by the author, 1970.

de Wolfe, Elsie. *The House in Good Taste*. New York: The Century Company, 1915.

Dubois, Jean. *Anne Orr Patchwork*. Durango, Colo.: La Plata Press, 1977.

Dunton, William Rush, Jr., M.D. *Old Quilts*. Catonsville, Md.: Published by the author, 1947.

Finley, Ruth E. *Old Patchwork Quilts and the Women Who Made Them*. Philadelphia and London: J.B. Lippincott, 1929.

Hall, Carrie A., and Kretsinger, Rose G. *The Romance of the Patchwork Quilt in America*. Caldwell, Idaho: Caxton Printers, 1935.

Havney, Andy Leon. "W.P.A. Handicrafts Rediscovered." *Historic Preservation Magazine* (July–September 1973).

Hillier, Bevis. *The Style of The Century, 1900–1980*. New York: E.P. Dutton, 1983.

Houck, Carter, and Miller, Myron. *American Quilts and How to Make Them*. New York: Charles Scribner's Sons, 1975.

Ickis, Marguerite. *The Standard Book of Quiltmaking and Collecting*. New York: Greystone Press, 1949.

Katz, Herbert, and Katz, Marjorie. *Museums U.S.A.* New York: Doubleday, 1965.

Kerber, Linda K., and Mathews, Jane De Hart. *Women's America: Refocusing the Past*. New York: Oxford University Press, 1982.

King, Elizabeth. *Quilting*. New York: Leisure League of America, 1934.

Ladies Art Company. *Quilt Patterns: Patchwork and Appliqué*. 1928 catalogue edition, and *Diagrams of Quilts, Sofa and Pin Cushion Patterns*. 1898. St. Louis, Missouri.

Leisure League of America. *Quilting*. 1934.

Lesieutre, Alain. *Art Nouveau*. New York: Paddington Press, 1974.

———. *The Spirit and Splendour of Art Deco*. New York: Paddington Press, 1974.

Marston, Gwen. *The Mary Schafer Quilt Collection*. Published by the author, 1980.

McClinton, Katharine Morrison. *Art Deco: A Guide for Collectors*. New York: Clarkson N. Potter, 1972.

*Modern Priscilla*. October 1928.

"Needlework Ideas." *Woman's Day*, 27 (September 1978).

Nelson, Cyril I., and Houck, Carter. *The Quilt Engagement Calendar Treasury*. New York: E.P. Dutton, 1982.

*1900–1910, This Fabulous Century*. vol. 1. New York: Time-Life Books, 1969.

Ninon. "Women Are Taking Up Quilting Again." *Chicago Daily News*, 1933.

Orlofsky, Patsy, and Orlofsky, Myron. *Quilts in America*. New York: McGraw-Hill, 1974.

Peto, Florence. *American Quilts and Coverlets*. New York: Chanticleer Press, 1949.

———. *Historic Quilts*. New York: American Historical Company, 1939.

*Quilter's Journal*. Joyce Gross, ed., Mill Valley, Calif.

*Quilter's Newsletter Magazine*. Bonnie Leman, ed., Wheatridge, Colo.: Leman Publications, 1969 to present.

Reif, Rita. "At Auction in 1983: Twentieth Century Soars." *The New York Times*, January 12, 1984.

Robertson, Elizabeth Wells. *American Quilts*. New York: The Studio Publications, 1948.

Safford, Carleton L., and Bishop, Robert. *America's Quilts and Coverlets*. New York: E.P. Dutton, 1972.

Sater, Joel. *The Patchwork Quilt*. Ephrata, Pa.: Science Press, 1981.

Sears, Roebuck and Company. *1902 Catalog*. New York: Bounty Books, 1969.

Selz, Peter, and Constantine, Mildred, eds. *Art Nouveau, Art and Design at the Turn of the Century*. New York: The Museum of Modern Art, 1975.

Sexton, Carlie. *Old-Fashioned Quilts*. Published by the author, 1928.

Shogren, Linda. *The Quilt Pattern Index*. San Mateo, Calif.: Pieceful Pleasures Publishers, 1981.

Snyder, Grace McCance. *No Time on My Hands, as told to Nellie S. Yost*. Caldwell, Idaho: The Caxton Printers, Ltd., 1963.

Stearns & Foster Company. *Catalogue of Quilt Pattern Designs and Needle Craft Supplies, Mountain Mist*. Cincinnati: undated.

———. *The Mountain Mist Blue Book of Prize Quilts*. Cincinnati: 1950.

———. *The 1957 Mountain Mist Blue Book of Quilts*. Cincinnati: 1956, 1966.

U.S. Department of Commerce, Bureau of the Census. *People of Rural America*. Washington, D.C., 1968.

U.S. Public Works Administration Project. *American Patchwork Quilts and Patterns*. South Langhorne/Croydon, Pennsylvania: Museum Extension Project. No date. This was published as a government document and was part of the WPA Index of American Design, 1935–1940.

Webster, Marie D. *Quilts; Their Story and How To Make Them*. New York: Doubleday, Page, 1915.

"What I See from New York." *The House Beautiful* (April 1930).

Woodard, Thos. K., and Greenstein, Blanche. *Crib Quilts and Other Small Wonders*. New York: E.P. Dutton, 1981.

———. *The Poster Book of Quilts*. New York: E.P. Dutton, 1984.

# REFERENCES

by Barbara Brackman, Lawrence, Kansas.
From: *An Encyclopedia of Pieced Quilt Patterns*
© 1983 by Barbara Brackman

AUTHORS' NOTE: Although some of the sources in the following material are duplicated in our bibliography, we preferred to keep Ms. Brackman's research intact, and so we present it here in full. This material is part of an ongoing project, to which new information is continually being added as it becomes available.

References which have an ° contain quilt patterns or are sources for full-size quilt patterns.

*The Quilt Pattern Index* by Linda Shogren (published by the author, 566 30th Ave., San Mateo, CA 94403) indexes many contemporary and still in-print sources and can tell you where to find a full-size pattern for a particular design.

Unless otherwise specified all sources are books.

ABC Publications. Published reprints of older patterns and new patterns. See *Little 'n' Big*.

*American Agriculturalist*. Periodical affiliated with Orange Judd Farmer 1847-1918.

° *Aunt Kate's Quilting Bee*. Periodical which was published from July, 1962 to Feb. 1980 in Oklahoma, Texas and Ohio.

° Aunt Martha Studios. Pamphlets and mail-order patterns are still offered by this source which began as the Colonial Pattern Co. in the early 1930's. The patterns were offered under the names Aunt Ellen, Betsy Ross and Aunt Matilda but the Aunt Martha name was most often seen. In 1935 Colonial Pattern began *Workbasket* magazine which offered the same patterns which were sold under Aunt Martha, so I have used the two names interchangeably. In 1949 Colonial Pattern and *Workbasket* split. Colonial Pattern has many of the Aunt Martha pamphlets in print. Current address: 340 West 5th St., Kansas City, MO. See *Workbasket*.

° Aunt Mattie. A 30's source from Milwaukee Comfort Mills, Milwaukee, WI.

Bacon, Lenice Ingram. *American Patchwork Quilts*, Wm. Morrow and Co., New York, 1973.

Baltimore Museum of Art. *The Great American Cover-Up: Counterpanes of the 18th & 19th Centuries*, Baltimore, MD., 1971. Catalog. Out of print.

° *Better Homes and Gardens* (periodical). Meredith Publishing Co., Des Moines, IA.

Betterton, Sheila. *Quilts and Coverlets from the American Museum in Britain*. Butler & Tanner, Ltd., London, 1978.

Beyer, Alice. *Quilting*. South Park Recreation Dept. Chicago, 1934. Reprinted by East Bay Heritage Quilters (PO Box 6223, Albany, CA 94706). Mostly Nancy Cabot patterns.

Beyer, Jinny. *Patchwork Patterns*. EPM Publications, McLean, VA, 1979.

Bishop, Robert & Patricia Coblentz. *New Discoveries in American Quilts*. E.P. Dutton, NY, 1975.

Bishop, Robert & Elizabeth Safanda, *A Gallery of Amish Quilts: Design Diversity from a Plain People*. E.P. Dutton, NY, 1976.

° Brown, Evelyn. *Tumbling Alley* (periodical). Published from ca. 1970 to 1981. Also wrote and published *Quilting: Do It My Way*, Gainesville, FL 1975.

° *Bureau Farmer* (periodical). From the American Farm Bureau Federation from 1925-35.

° Burnham, Dorothy. *Pieced Quilts of Ontario*. Royal Ontario Museum, Toronto, 1975. Catalog.

° Cabot, Nancy. Syndicated column written by Loretta Leitner Rising for the *Chicago Tribune* in the 30's. The Cabot patterns were mail-order and sold in pamphlets which were sold under the Spinning Wheel Co. name. The same patterns were also offered by *Progressive Farmer* magazine (see entry). The column began in 1932 and continued through the decade. Nancy Cabot patterns are reprinted in a number of publications including those available from

Bannister, Barbara, Alanson, MI 49706.

Goodspeed, Sally. *Quiltmaker's Time*, 2318 N. Charles St., Baltimore, MD 21218.

Smith, Wilma, *Nancy's*. Box 155, Crawfordsville, OR 97336.

Van Das, Edna. *Dutch Girl Scrapbooks*, Box 145, Crete, IL 60417.

° *Canada Quilts* (periodical). Published ca. 1970 to present. 13 Pinewood Ave., Grimsby, Ontario, Canada L3M-1W2.

° *Capper's Weekly* (periodical). Capper Publications, 616 Jefferson, Topeka, KS 66607 has published *Capper's Weekly* since 1879. From 1927 through 1935 they offered mail-order patterns by staff member Louise Fowler Roote and at least one pamphlet (Whittemore, Margaret. *Quilting: A New/Old Art* n.d.). Since the 40's they have offered mail-order pamphlets which are published by Famous Features syndicate and advertised in a number of other publications also. These pamphlets include some of the patterns from the Roote column. Other Capper Publications which included the same patterns as in *Capper's Weekly* were *Kansas Farmer, Mail and Breeze, Household, Household Magazine*, and *Missouri Ruralist*. See Famous Features.

Caulfield, Sophia Frances Anne & Blanche C. Saward. *The Dictionary of Needlework*. Original copyright 1882. Reprinted by Arno Press, 1972.

° Clark, Grandmother. A series of pamphlets published by the WLM Clark Inc. Co., which sold thread during the 30's. Clark merged with J.P. Coats to become Coats and Clark which is also known as the Spool Cotton Co. (see both these entries). Patterns which appeared in Grandmother Clark booklets also appeared in Grandmother Dexter pamphlets. Grandmother Clark reprints are available from Barbara Bannister, Alanson, MI 49706.

The pamphlets are the following:
#19 *Grandmother Clark's Patchwork Quilts*
#20 *Grandmother's Patchwork Quilt Designs*
#21 *Grandmother's Oldfashioned Quilt Designs*
#22 *Grandmother Clark's Quilting Designs* (no patchwork)
#23 *Grandmother's Authentic Early American Patchwork Quilts*

Clarke, Mary Washington. *Kentucky Quilts and Their Makers*, University Press of Kentucky, Lexington, KY, 1976.

° Coats and Clark. Also known as the Spool Cotton Co. Originally two separate thread manufacturers: J.P. Coats and WLM Clark. See Grandmother Clark and Spool Cotton Co.

Colby, Averil.
*Patchwork*, Chas, T. Branford, Co., Newton Centre, MA, 1958.
*Patchwork Quilts*, Scribner's, NY, 1965.

° *Comfort Magazine*. (Periodical 1888– ca. 1930). Augusta, Maine. Published by Vickery Publishing Co. which also published *Hearth and Home* (see entry), and patterns which appeared in one magazine often appeared in others. For reprints of *Comfort* patterns contact Wilma Smith, PO Box 155, Crawfordsville, OR 97336. There was at least one pamphlet from *Comfort* called *Comfort's Applique and Patchwork: Revival of Old Time Patchwork* ca. 1920.

° *Country Gentleman* (periodical). Founded as *Gennessee Farmer* in the early 19th century, it became *Country Gentleman* in 1853; changed to *Better Farming* in 1955; merged with *Farm Journal* in 1955 and is currently publishing under the name of *Country Gentleman* again.

° *Country Home* (periodical). Published in New York, NY, which offered mail order patterns which were probably syndicated. The pattern I have seen is dated 1933 and is not easily recognized as one from a common syndicate.

° *Country Life* (periodical). Published near the turn of the century.

*Craft Horizons* (periodical). Still being published. Originated ca. 1940.

*Dakota Farmer* (periodical). Established 1881 from Aberdeen S.D. Had a thriving regional quilt column in the late 20's.

° Danneman, Barbara. *Step by Step Quiltmaking*. Golden Press, Western Publishing Co., Racine, WI, 1974.

° Danner, Scioto Imhoff and Helen Ericson. A mail-order pattern source known as Mrs. Danner's Quilts, originated by Danner in 1934 and sold to Ericson in 1970. There were four pamphlets printed by Danner and Ericson has added four more. All currently available from Mrs. Danner's Quilts, Box 650, Emporia, KS 66801.

Davison, Mildred. *American Quilts 1819-1948 from the Museum Collection*, Art Institute of Chicago, 1959, Catalog. Out of Print.

DeGraw, Imelda. See Denver Art Museum.

Denver Art Museum has published two museum catalogs:
DeGraw, Imelda. *Quilts and Coverlets*, 1974.
Dunham, Lydia Roberts. Denver Art Museum Quilt Collection. *Denver Art Museum Winter Quarterly*, 1963. Out of Print.

° *Detroit Free Press* (periodical). Patterns appeared in the 20's and 30's. They were primarily syndicated but some idiosyncratic patterns apparently appeared.

° *Detroit News*/Public Service Bureau Home Newspaper. Quilt Pattern column in mid 30's by Marian Morris Goodman. Reprints available from 90 Zils Rd., La Selva Beach, CA 950767.

° Dexter, Grandma. A series of pamphlets (ca. 1930) from the Virginia Snow Studios which was part of the Dexter Yarn and Thread Co. in Elgin, IL. Some of these patterns were identical to Grandmother Clark patterns (see entry).

The pamphlets are the following:
# 36 *Grandma Dexter's Appliqué and Patchwork Quilt Designs*
#36a *Grandma Dexter's Appliqué and Patchwork Designs*
#36b *Grandma Dexter's New Appliqué and Patchwork Designs*

° Doyle, Joseph. The Joseph Doyle Co. printed at least two pamphlets offering mail-order patterns. The *Patchworker's Companion* (1911) and *Patchwork and Quilt Making*, Clinton Hill Station, Newark, N.J. (no date).

° DuBois, Jean, editor and publisher of LaPlata Press which has published the following:
*Bye Baby Bunting*, 1979.
*A Galaxy of Stars: America's Favorite Quilts*, 1976.
*The Wool Quilt*, 1978.
*LaPlata Letter* (periodical) published from ca. 1977 to present.
plus reprints of other out-of-print patterns. Current address: Evans, CO 80620-0820.

Dunham, Lydia Roberts. See Denver Art Museum.

Dunton, William Rush, Jr., M.D. *Old Quilts*, printed by the author, Catonsville, MD, 1946.

° Elwood, Judy, Joyce Tennery and Alice Richardson. *Tennessee Quilting: Designs plus Patterns*, published by the authors, Oak Ridge, TN, 1982.

Ericson, Helen. See Danner/Ericson

° *Evangeline's*. A column in the St. John, New Brunswick (Canada) newspaper in the 20's and 30's.

Fadely, Jean. *Frameless Quilt Making for Beginners*. Published by the author, 1971.

° Famous Features. A syndicated, mail-order pattern source. Current address is 1150 Ave. of the Americas, NY, NY 10036. Pamphlets offered in a number of periodicals. Some of the patterns are originally from *Capper's Weekly* (see entry). Current author is Mabel Obenchain.

° *Farm and Fireside* (periodical) published by Crowell, Springfield, OH. Patterns appeared in first third of 20th century.

° *Farm Journal* (periodical). Began in March 1877 and is still publishing. FJ has absorbed at least three other older quilt pattern sources (*Country Gentleman, The Farmer's Wife* and *Household Journal*—see entries). Over the years the periodical has offered mail-order patterns and pamphlets. Some of the patterns are reproduced in Martens, Rachel, *Modern Patchwork*, Countryside Press, (a division of *Farm Journal*, Inc.) copyright © 1970. 230 W. Washington Square, Philadelphia, PA.

° *Farmer's Wife, The*. A periodical which was published in St. Paul, MN from the 19th century through 1939 when it merged with *Farm Journal* (see entry). Patterns were sold in at least 2 pamphlets (Orrine Johnson and Eleanor Lewis, *The Farmer's Wife Book of Quilts*, 1931. Leonore Dunnigan, *Quilts*, St. Paul ca. 1930) Reprints available from Barbara Bannister, Alanson, MI 49706.

Finley, Ruth. *Old Patchwork Quilts and the Women Who Made Them*. J.B. Lippincott, Philadelphia, PA, 1929.

° Frank, Robert. *E-Z Patterns for Patchwork and Applique Quilts*, Kalamazoo, MI, ca. 1940.

° Gammell, Alice I., *Polly Prindle's Book of American Patchwork Quilts*. Grosset & Dunlap, NY, 1973. Reprinted by Dover Publications.

*Godey's Lady's Book* (periodical) published in Philadelphia 1830–1898.

° Golden Hands. Farnsworth, Ruth and Carol Collins, *Patchwork and Applique*, Golden Hands, Marshall Cavendish, London, 1976.

Goodman, Liz and Stephanie Miller, *All About Patchwork: Golden Hands Special #10*, Marshall Cavendish, London, 1973.

° Goodspeed, Sally. *Quiltmaker's Time*. Books 1 & 2. Old Patterns and some originals. Nancy Cabot reprints. 2318 N. Charles St., Baltimore, MD 21218.

° *Good Housekeeping* (periodical). The Hearst Corp. 959 Eighth Ave., NY NY 10019. Anne Orr was needlework editor in early 20th century (see Anne Orr).

Graeff, Marie Knorr. *Pennsylvania German Quilts*. Home Craft Course, Volume XIV, Mrs. D. Naaman Keiper, Kutztown, PA 1946.

Gutcheon Beth, *The Perfect Patchwork Primer*, David McKay Co., Inc., NY, 1973.

° Gutcheon, Beth & Jeffrey Gutcheon, *The Quilt Design Workbook*, Rawson Assoc. NY, 1976.

Haders, Phyllis, *Sunshine & Shadow: The Amish and their Quilts*. The Main Street Press, Clinton, NJ, 1976.

Hall, Carrie A. and Rose G. Kretsinger. *The Romance of the Patchwork Quilt in America*, Caxton Printers, Caldwell, ID, 1935.

° Harris, Della. A mail-order source for patterns ca. 1930. 2011 N. 7th St., Waco, TX. Pamphlet contained some McKim patterns and some not seen elsewhere.

° Hartman, Marie. *Quilts, Quilts...* A pamphlet published by the author, PO Box 25402, Tampa, FL 33603, 1980.

Heard, Audrey and Beverly Pryor. *The Complete Guide to Quilting*. Creative Home Library (*Better Homes and Gardens*) Des Moines, IA, 1974.

*Hearth and Home* (periodical) published by the Vickery Publishing Co., Augusta ME, 1868–1933. Vickery also published *Comfort* (see entry). Clara Stone submitted many of the *Hearth and Home* patterns and they are also included in her booklet (see entry). Some *Hearth and Home* patterns are reprinted in the following:

Bannister, Barbara and Edna Paris Ford. *The United States Patchwork Pattern Book*, Dover Publishing Co., New York, 1976.

Bannister, Barbara and Edna Paris Ford, *State Capitals Quilt Blocks*, Dover Publishing Co., New York, 1977.

Smith, Wilma, *Quilt Designs from Hearth and Home*, Published by the author, PO Box 155, Crawfordsville, OR., 97336.

° Heath, Thelma G. *How to Make a Really Different Quilt*, pamphlet, published by the author, ca. 1940.

° Herrschner, Frederick. Frederick Herrschner, Inc. is a mail-order source from the early 20th century in Chicago. Pamphlets include: *Quilts: Beautiful Designs for Applique, Embroidery: Authentic Reproductions for Patchwork*.

Hinson, Delores A. *Quilting Manual*, Hearthside Press, Inc. NY, 1966. Has been reprinted by Dover Publications.

*A Quilter's Companion*, Arco, NY, 1973.

Holstein, Jonathan. *Abstract Design in American Quilts*. Whitney Museum of Art, NY, 1971. Catalog, out of print.

*American Pieced Quilts*, Viking Press, NY, 1973.

*The Pieced Quilt*, New York Graphic Society, Greenwich, CT, 1973.

° Home Art Studios. A mail-order pattern source. Patterns appeared under the name Colonial Quilts, Bettina, Hope Winslow and others in over 90 periodicals from the 1930's. The Home Art Studios were located in Des Moines, Iowa and owned by H. Ver Mehren. Although they used a name similar to Colonial Pattern Co. they were not affiliated with Aunt Martha Studios, nor were they associated with *Needlecraft/Home Arts Magazine* (see entries).

Some of the Home Art Studio catalogs:

*The Needleart Vogue*

*Hope Winslow's Quilt Book*

*Colonial Quilts*

*Master Quilting Album—101 Favorite Quilting Designs*

*Aunt Mary Jacob's Album of Favorite Quilting Designs*

*Mary Fowler's Album of Favorite Quilting Designs*

*Master Album of 101 Favorite Quilting Designs*

° *Household Journal* (periodical). Published in Springfield, OH in the early 20th century by Crowell which also

published *Farm and Fireside* (see entry). Patterns were sold under the name Aunt Jane. *Household Journal* later moved to Batavia, IL and was published as *Household Management Journal*. Later absorbed by *Farm Journal* (see entry). Pamphlets (*Aunt Jane's Quilt Pattern Book*, no date, and *Aunt Jane's Prize Winning Quilt Designs*, 1914, which has been reprinted by Aunt Jane's, 90 Zils Rd., La Selva Beach, CA 95076.)
° *Household Magazine*. See *Capper's Weekly*.
° Ickis, Marguerite. *The Standard Book of Quilt Making and Collecting*, Grey Stone Press, 1949. Reprinted by Dover Publications, 1959.
James, Michael. *The Quiltmaker's Handbook: A Guide to Design and Construction*. A Spectrum Book, Prentice Hall, Englewood Cliffs, NJ, 1978.
Johnson, Bruce. *A Child's Comfort: Baby and Doll Quilts in American Folk Art*. Harcourt Brace Jovanovich, NY, 1977.
° Johnson, Mary Elizabeth. *Prize Country Quilts*. Birmingham, AL, Oxmoor House, a division of *Progressive Farmer*, 1977. Winners in a 1976 PF block contest. See *Progressive Farmer*.
° *KCS Kansas City Star*. Patterns appeared in periodicals (*Kansas City Star*, *Weekly Kansas City Star* and *Weekly Star Farmer*) from 1928–1960. Earlier patterns were syndicated McKim patterns but in the early 30's the periodicals began printing old and original patterns by staff members and readers. Reprints are available from Barbara Bannister, Alanson, MI 49706 and from Betty McAdams, 7801 Morris Dr., Little Rock, Ark. 72209.
Khin, Yvonne M. *The Collector's Dictionary of Quilt Names and Patterns*. Acropolis Books, Washington DC, 1980.
° *LAC Ladies Art Co.* catalogs. The Ladies Art Co. was a mail-order pattern source which reprinted patterns that were shown in other periodicals of the time as well as some that were apparently original with the company. The original catalog, titled *Diagrams of Quilt, Sofa and Pin Cushion Patterns*, was printed in 1898 and included pieced and appliqué patterns numbered 1 through 420. Cuesta Benberry writes me that she *thinks* the catalog was reprinted in 1907 with numbers to 450, in 1922 with numbers to 500 and she has a copy of a 1928 edition titled *Quilt Patterns: Patchwork and Appliqué* with patterns numbered 1 through 530. She believes another edition was printed in the 30's with patterns 1–544.

Occasionally a pattern was dropped from the later editions of the catalog or a new pattern substituted with the same number, but generally the patterns can be dated by their numbers. The company was managed by H. M. Brockstedt in St. Louis. The 1928 catalog has been reprinted in a pamphlet called *700 Olde Time Needlecraft Designs and Patterns* available from the House of White Birches, PO Box 337, Seabrook, NH 03874.
° *LCPQ Lady's Circle Patchwork Quilt* (periodical). Published from 1973 through the present. Carter Houck, editor. 21 West 26th St., NY, NY 10010
° *Ladies Home Journal* (periodical). Began as *Ladies Journal and Practical Housekeeper* in 1883 and has published patterns until present. In the first two decades of the 20th century Marie Webster was an editor. Several of the patterns shown in her book were also in the magazine. See Webster.
Lithgow, Marilyn. *Quiltmaking and Quiltmakers*. Funk & Wagnalls, N.Y., 1974.

° *Little 'n' Big* (periodical). Published from February 1964 through March 1966. Betty Flack was editor.
° Lockport Batting Co., Lockport N.Y. In addition to selling quilting supplies the company sold patterns during the 30's and 40's. At least 2 pamphlets were printed (*Replicas of Famous Quilts, Old and New*, 1942 and *The Lockport Quilt Pattern Book* – no date) which contain essentially the same patterns. Lockport sold many of the Anne Orr patterns (see entry).
° Mahler, Celine Blanchard. *Once Upon a Quilt*, Van Nostrand Reinhold, NY, 1973.
*Maritime Farmer, The.* (periodical). Published in St. John's, New Brunswick, Canada, ca. 1935.
Marshall, Martha. *Quilts of Appalachia: The Mountain Woman and her Quilts*. Tri-city Printing, Co., Bluff City, TN 37618, 1972.
° McCall's. McCall's publishing company has been offering patterns over a long period of time. To distinguish between older patterns offered through the magazine and a recent series of booklets I have used the following references:
*McCall's Magazine.* Patterns which were pictured in the periodical in the 20's, 30's and 40's which could be bought by mail order.
McCall's. A series of booklets with patterns included in them was published from 1972 through 1975. Some of the information was reprinted from the magazine in the 50's and 60's, and some was original information on old and new quilt patterns. These booklets have, in turn, been reprinted as *McCall's Book of Quilts*, Simon and Schuster/The McCall Pattern Co., NY, 1975.
° McElwain, Mary A. Mail-order pattern source from Mary A. McElwain Quilt Shop in Walworth, Wisconsin, which published at least one pamphlet, *The Romance of Village Quilts* in 1936. This was later reprinted by Rock River Cotton Co., Janesville, WI, ca. 1955.
McKendry, Ruth. *Quilts and Other Bedcoverings in the Canadian Tradition*. Van Nostrand, Reinhold, Toronto, 1979.
° McKim, Ruby Short. McKim Studios in Independence, MO, was a mail-order source for patterns. McKim also syndicated a newspaper column with actual full-size patterns in the 20's and 30's. At least four pamphlets were printed (*Designs Worth Doing, Adventures in Needlecraft, Adventures in Home Beautifying* and *101 Patchwork Patterns*). The latter has been reprinted by Dover Publications, N.Y., 1962.
Meeker, L. K. *Quilt Patterns for the Collector*. Published by the author, 3145 NE 27th, Portland OR 97212, 1979.
Mills, Susan Winter. *Illustrated Index to Traditional American Quilt Patterns*. Arco Publishing Co., NY, 1980.
° Mitchell, V. Jean. *Quilt Kansas*. Spencer Museum of Art, Lawrence, KS, 1978.
° *Modern Priscilla* (periodical). Begun in 1887, it offered mail-order patterns. It was absorbed by *Needlecraft—The Home Arts Magazine* (see entry) in 1930.
° Mountain Mist. The Stearns & Foster Co. was begun in Cincinnati, OH, in 1846. It has offered mail-order patterns since the 20's. Until 1976 it enclosed patterns with its quilt-batting packaging. It recently began selling patterns in quilt shops. At least three pamphlets have been published (*The Mountain Mist Blue Book of Quilts*, 1935, *The 1957 Mountain Mist Blue Book of Quilts* and Edwards, Phoebe, *Anyone Can Quilt*, 1975).

Most of their 130 patterns are still available from the company.
- *NNT–Nimble Needle Treasures* (periodical) edited by Patricia Almy, in Sapulpa, Oklahoma from 1969 through 1975.

Nebraska Collections. *Quilts from Nebraska Collections.* Catalog of an exhibition organized by the Lincoln Quilters Guild and the University of Nebraska Art Gallery. No date, ca. 1975, out of print.
- Needlecraft refers to *Needlecrafts/The Home Arts Magazine* which was published by the Vickery Publishing Co. in Augusta, ME from ca. 1910 to 1941. Originally called *Needlecraft/The Home Arts Magazine*, it changed its name to *Home-Arts/Needlecraft*. It absorbed *Modern Priscilla* (see entry) in 1930. It offered mail-order patterns throughout its history.
- OCS Old Chelsea Station Needlecraft Service. Mail-order, syndicated pattern source from the early 1930's until the present. Patterns were advertised widely (and still are) in periodicals under the names Alice Brooks and Laura Wheeler as well as lesser-known names such as Carol Curtis. Pamphlets are currently available but these do not include the majority of the early Brooks/Wheeler patterns. The address of the company had always been the Old Chelsea Station post office in New York. Currently the address is Box 84, Old Chelsea Station, NY, NY 10013. For reprints of some of the older patterns contact Wilma Smith, Box 155, Crawfordsville, OR 97336.

Ohio Farmer (periodical). Began as *The Ohio Practical Farmer* ca. 1810, published by The Lawrence Publishing Co., Cleveland, OH. Had a flourishing pattern column in the 1890's.
- *Oklahoma Farmer Stockman* (periodical). Published in Oklahoma City, OK. In the late 20's and early 30's had a column entitled Good Cheer Quilt Patterns.

*Orange Judd Farmer, The Western Edition of The American Agriculturalist*, begun ca. 1870, published in Chicago. Flourishing pattern column in the 1890's.
- Orbelo, Beverly Ann, *A Texas Quilting Primer.* Corona Publishing Co., San Antonio TX, 1980.

Orlofsky, Patsy, and Myron Orlofsky. *Quilts in America.* McGraw-Hill, NY, 1974.
- Orr, Anne. A designer of quilt and other needlework patterns in the early 20th century. She was an editor at *Good Housekeeping* (see entry). Her patterns later appeared under the Lockport Batting Co. name (see entry) but for many years they were sold as Anne Orr Patterns. Jean DuBois has published *Anne Orr Patchwork* which contains reprints of some of her patterns (see entry).
- Page, Nancy. A syndicated column written by Florence LaGanke which appeared in many periodicals ca. 1925–1940. Patterns were mail order. Reprints available from Barbara Bannister, Alanson, MI 49706.
- Penny, Prudence. The name for the quilt column in the *Seattle Post-Intelligencer* in the 20's and 30's. There seem to have been a number of artists; some are signed M. Buren; some are McKim syndicated columns (see entry), and some are unsigned. The newspaper column printed patterns, sold them mail-order and there was at least one pamphlet (*Old Time Quilts, Seattle Post-Intelligencer,* 1927).
- *People's Popular Monthly* (periodical). Published from 1896–1931; absorbed *Ladies Favorite Magazine* in 1908.

Peterson's Magazine (periodical). Begun in 1842 as *Lady's World of Fashion*; in 1849 changed to *Peterson's Magazine.* Merged with *Argosy* in 1894.

Peto, Florence. *American Quilts and Coverlets*, Chanticleer Press, Inc., NY, 1949. *Historic Quilts.* American Historical Co., Inc. NY, 1939.
- Pforr, Effie Chalmers, *Award Winning Quilts*, Oxmoor House, a Division of *Progressive Farmer*, Birmingham, AL, 1974. Prize Winners in a 1973 *Progressive Farmer* (see entry) block contest.
- *Prairie Farmer* (periodical). Printed in Chicago, published at least one pamphlet (Schenk, Lois [ed], *Quilt Booklet #1*, ca. 1931). Mail-order patterns.
- *Progressive Farmer.* Periodical published in Birmingham, AL (820 Shades Creek Parkway) since 1895. During the 30's and 40's sold mail-order patterns from The Spinning Wheel Co., which were similar to Nancy Cabot patterns (see entry), and I have referred to most PF patterns as Nancy Cabot. The patterns were sold mail-order under the name of Betty Jones. Some of the older patterns have been reprinted in the following books: Hill, Sallie. *One Dozen Quilt Patterns, Progressive Farmer*, 1946. *Heirloom Quilts to Treasure. Progressive Farmer*, Oxmoor House, Birmingham AL, 1931. See also Mary Elizabeth Johnson and Effie Chalmers Pforr for recent PF quilt-contest winners published in book form.
- QEC Nelson, Cyril I. *The Quilt Engagement Calendar.* A series begun in 1975 which includes photographs of museum-quality quilts. The patterns for a few of the quilts are included in Nelson, Cyril I., and Carter Houck, *The Quilt Engagement Calendar Treasury*, E.P. Dutton, NY, 1982.
- QNL or QNM *Quilter's Newsletter Magazine* (periodical) published by Leman Publications, PO Box 394, Wheatridge CO, 80038, edited by Bonnie Leman, published from 1969 through the present. Includes a mail-order pattern service which was at one time called Heirloom Plastics.
- QW *Quilt World* (periodical) published by The House of White Birches, Box 337, Seabrook, NH 03874; published from 1976 through present.
- *Quilt* (periodical) published by Harris Publications, 79 Madison Ave., NY, NY 10016. Published since 1978.

Robertson, Elizabeth Wells. *American Quilts.* Studio Publications, Inc., NY, 1948.
- *Rural New Yorker* (periodical) from Rural Publishing Co., NY. Begun in 1841, published through the mid 20th century. Quilt column thrived from 1930 through 1937, written by Mrs. R.E. Smith, who mentioned once it was a syndicated column, although I have not seen it in any other publications.

Safford, Carleton L. and Robert Bishop. *America's Quilts and Coverlets.* E.P. Dutton, N.Y., 1972.
- Sears, Roebuck and Co., *Century of Progress in Quilt Making.* Chicago, 1934. Pamphlet featuring winners of their contest held in conjunction with the 1933 World's Fair.
- Sexton, Carlie. A mail-order pattern source from Wheaton, IL. which published at least three pamphlets (*Old Fashioned Quilts*, published by the author, Wheaton, IL, 1928, *Yesterday's Quilts in Homes of Today*, Meredith Publishing Co., Des Moines, 1930 and *How to Make a Quilt*, published by the author, Wheaton, IL, 1932). Carlie Sexton's patterns and pamphlets have

been reproduced by Barbara Bannister, Alanson, MI 49706.

Shelburne. Carlisle, Lilian Baker. *Pieced Work and Applique Quilts at Shelburne Museum*, Shelburne, VT, 1957. Catalog, currently available.

° Shogren, Linda, *The Drunkard's Path Quilt Compendium*, published by the author, Pieceful Pleasures, 566 30th Ave., San Mateo CA 94403, 1978.

*The Fan Quilt Compendium.* Published by the author, San Mateo, CA, 1979.

*The Log Cabin Quilt Compedium.* Published by the author, San Mateo, CA, 1977.

Spool Cotton Co. Another name for the Coats and Clark Co. which manufactured thread and sold patterns. See J. P. Coats and WLM Clark. Published at least two pamphlets in the 40's (*Quilts*, S-22, 1945 and *Quilts* #190, 1942).

Stone, Clara A. *Practical Needlework: Quilt Patterns*, C.W. Calkins & Co., Boston, 1910. A pamphlet which was one of a series on needlework. Stone had contributed many patterns to *Hearth and Home* (see entry) and patterns from the magazine are included in this pamphlet.

° *Successful Farming* (periodical). Published by the Meredith Corp., Des Moines, IA. Began publishing in 1902 and continued through the middle of this century. Carlie Sexton (see entry) wrote for them.

° Taylor Bedding Manufacturing Co., Taylor, TX has published the following pamphlets *31 Quilt Designs by Taylor-Made* ca. 1940 (has many designs similar to Grandma Dexter (see entry)) and *Barbara Taylor's Quilting for Fun and Profit*.

University of Kansas. The art museum at the University of Kansas has published two catalogs, both of which are out of print.

*One Hundred Years of American Quilts.* University of Kansas, Museum of Art, 1973.

*Quilter's Choice*, Helen Foresman Spencer Museum of Art, University of Kansas, Lawrence, Kansas 66045, 1978.

*Valley Farmer* (periodical). One clipping I have seen is ca. 1910.

Vote, Marjean. *Patchwork Pleasure: A Pattern Identification Guide.* Wallace Homestead, Des Moines, IA, 1960. Out of print.

° Walker Patterns. The patterns, signed Mary Evangeline Walker, were syndicated in newspapers and available through the mail in the 30's. Mail was addressed to Lydia LeBaron Walker.

*Wallace's Farmer* (periodical). Published in Des Moines, IA, from 1874 through middle of this century. A good source of patterns in the 1890's.

° Webster, Marie D. *Quilts: Their Story and How To Make Them.* Tudor Publishing Co., NY, 1915. See *Ladies Home Journal*.

° Winthrop, Hetty. Syndicated column in the 30's distributed by Bell Syndicate, NY.

° *Woman's Circle* (periodical). Published in the 60's; occasionally had patterns.

° *Woman's Day* (periodical). Has included quilt patterns from the 40's to the present. Some of the articles on quilts were compiled in: Lane, Rose Wilder, *Woman's Day Book of American Needlework*, Simon & Schuster, NY, 1962.

*Woman's Home Companion* (periodical). Began in 1866 as *Ladies' Home Companion*. Changed name in 1899.

° *Woman's World* (periodical). Published by The Manning Publishing Co., Chicago, in the 20's and 30's. Patterns were sold mail-order. At least one pamphlet published (*The Patchwork Book*, 1931).

Woodard, Thomas K. and Blanche Greenstein. *Crib Quilts and Other Small Wonders.* E.P. Dutton, NY, 1981.

Wooster, Ann Sargent. *Quiltmaking: The Modern Approach to a Traditional Craft.* Drake, NY, 1972.

° *Workbasket* (periodical). Begun in 1935 by Colonial Pattern Co. (see Aunt Martha); it was affiliated with the Aunt Martha Studios until 1949 when *Workbasket* and Colonial Pattern Co. split. *Workbasket* is currently published by Modern Handcrafts, 3958 Central St., Kansas City, MO. The magazine published many quilt patterns until the early 50's; it no longer publishes them. Most *Workbasket* patterns were also sold as Aunt Martha patterns, and I have referred to them under that name.

# INDEX

Page references for illustrations are in **boldface** type.

"Airplanes," **64**
"Album," **122**
Alice Brooks (syndicated columnist), 51, 67, 83
"Alphabet," **129**
"American Beauty Bouquet," **54**
American Glory, 15
*American Home*, 18
*American Home Pattern Book*, 34
American Indians, 114, 118
"American Life," **115**
*American Peasant Art, The*, 10
*American Quilts*, 12
*American Quilts and Coverlets*, 12
Amish quilts and quilters, 10, 17, 35, **70**, 76, **79**, 97
Andres, Emma, 23, 29, **56**, 119
appliqué technique, **ii**, **x**, 5, 10, 12, 13, 14, 16, 17, **19**, 21, 25, 26, **28**, **43**, **48**, **52**, **53**, **54**, **57**, **61**, **62**, **63**, **64**, **65**, **66**, **67**, 76, **79**, **80**, **81**, **82**, **83**, **88**, **99**, **101**, **103**, **104**, 118, **120**, **121**, **123**, **124**, **130**, **133**
"The Army Star," 16
Art Institute of Chicago, 5, **121**
Artano Thread Co., 34
"Astrology," **127**
Aunt Martha Studios (syndicate), 11, 16, 17, 21, 23, 24, **132**

"Baby Chrysanthemum," **50**
"Balloons," **95**
"Baltimore Album," 10, 12, 25
"Bambi," **132**
Barrier, Mittie, **124**
"Basket of Flower" quilts, **79**, **81**
"Basket of Roses," **80**
"Baskets of Star Flowers," **82**
Batting companies, 21
Beard, Eleanor, 25
"The Beautiful Unequaled Gardens of Eden and Elenale," **114**
Benberry, Cuesta, 31, 37
*Better Homes & Gardens*, 20
"Blackwork," 33
"Blue Eagle," 14, 16
"Blue Iris," 50
"Bouquet of Pansies," **52**
Bowen, Arsinoe Kelsey, **ii**, **62**
Brachman, Barbara, 37
"Broken Circles," **93**
"Broken Dishes," **110**
"Broken Star," **76**
Brown, Dovie, **108**
"Butterflies," **66**
Butterick, 18

Caden, Margaret Rogers, 24
Calvert, Moneca, 25
*Capper's Weekly*, 24, **44**, **76**, **107**, **108**
"Caroline's Quilt," 13

"Carpenter's Wheel," **77**
"Casper the Ghost," **132**
*Cassell's Illustrated Family Paper*, 18
"Center Diamond," **97**
"Center Medallion," **x**, 18
Century of Progress Exposition, 1, 12, 14, 23, 24, **24**, 36, **92**, **104**, **106**
*Century of Progress in Quilting*, 24
"Century of Progress" quilts, **89**, **90**, **104**
Challie de Mousseline, 10
Chaney, Anna, 18
Chapman, Suzanne, 5
Chappell, Mildred Jacob, **116**
"Charm" quilts, 31, **93**
"Checkerboard Baskets," **82**
"Checkerboard Vortex," **93**
"Cherry Tree" quilts, 12, **125**
*Chicago Daily News*, 9
*Chicago Tribune*, 5, 21, **50**, **96**
"Chief's Blanket," **95**
"Chinese Coins," **97**
Clamshell quilting, **85**
"Clamshells," **106**
"Cloth Picture Books," 34
Cochran, F., **113**
"Coffee Cups," **64**
Colonial American heritage, 7
"Colonial Rose," 24
*Comfort Magazine*, 23, 34
"Compass and Wreath," **76**
Continental Quilting Congress, 12
"Cottage Garden," **62**
Cotton prints, **27**, **28**
"Country Gardens," **46**
*Country Gentlemen, The*, 34
"Covered Bridge," **118**
"The Cranes," **126**
"Crazy" quilts, 7, 10, 18, 29, **123**, **124**
Cross-stitch embroidery, 11, 33–34, **47**, **58**, **86**
"Cross-stitch Garden," **47**
"Cross-stitch Sampler," **86**
Cutout-motif quilts, 31

Daingerfield, Miss Bessie, 26
"Dancing Daffodils," **48**
Danner, Mrs. Scioto, 1, 5, 12, 14, 20, 23, **79**
Deibert, Joseph P., 33
Depression, 5, 35, **84**, **100**
*Depression quilt*, 5
Designs:
  Art Deco style, 11, 13, 14, 35, **59**, **67**, **72**, **73**, **76**, **95**, **97**, **137**
  Art Nouveau style, 11, 14, **15**, 35, **80**, **125**
  commercial, 13, 18, **50**, **57**, **58**
  derivation of, 12–13
  historical, 12–13
  inspiration for, 13–14
  marketing of, 11
  precursors of Pop Art, 31, **63**, **85**
*Designs Worth Doing*, 14

*Detroit Free Press, The*, 34
de Wolfe, Elsie, 7–8
*Diagrams of Quilt, Sofa and Pin Cushion Patterns*, 20
Dickerson, E. R., 33
"Dicky Bird," **67**
"Donkey," **100**
"Double Wedding Ring" quilts, 5, **68**, **70**, **73**
"Dresden Plate," **2**, 5, 33
Dunton, William, Dr., 9–10, 12, 35
"Early American" (quilt kit), **22**
East Lincoln Christian Church, 71
Easterly, Charles, 33
"Eastern Star," **74**
Eastern States Exposition, 23
Eccentric quilts, 29, 31
Edwards, Phoebe, 21
"Eight-Point Combination Feathered Star," 24
Eisfeller, Pine Hawkes, 12, 18, **49**, **62**
"Eleanor Roosevelt Album," **103**
"Elephant," **100**
"The Elephant's Child," **131**
*Encyclopedia of Pieced Quilt Patterns*, 37
Entrepreneurs, 11
Evans, Mary, 25

Fabrics, 8
"Fanny's Fan," 10
"Fans" quilts, **71–72**
*Farm and Fireside*, 13, 16, 23
"Fashion Ladies," **88**
"Fauna and Flora," **124**
"FDR's Election," **101**
Feed-sack quilt, **31**, 32
"Field of Daisies," **44**
Figaro, Ruth Easton, 92
Finley, Ruth, 5, 11–12, 26, 31, **63**
"Flag," **99**
Flour-sack quilt, 32
"Flower Basket Petit Point," **111**, **112**
"Flower Baskets," **81**
"Flowers and Lattice," **48**
"Flowers in a Vase," **56**
Forney, Mrs. G. M., 13
Fortner, Myrtle Mae, **117**
Fox, Mrs. Charles G. **101**
"French Baskets," **79**
"Friendship Fan," **71**
"Friendship Wheel," **70**
"Funny Papers," **128**

Gay, Pocahontas Virginia, **122**
"George Washington's Birthday," **99**
Gimbel's, **127**
"Glorious Lady Freedom," 25
"God's Autumn Cover," 33
*Godey's Lady's Book*, 21
Gold Art Needlework Company, 23, **54**
"The Golden Star," 23
*Good Housekeeping*, 1, 11, 16, 20, 21, 24, **46**

147

Grandma Dexter, **96**
Grandmother Clark, **106**
"Grandmother's Flower Garden" quilts, 5, 29, **107, 108**
Grandmother's Quilt Patterns (syndicated column), **45**
"Grapevine", **51**
Great American Quilt Contest, 25
Greenaway, Kate, 31, 33, 34
Greiner, Caroline Charlotta, 13
"Gypsy Trail"/"Snake in the Hollow," 73

Hagerman, Betty, **30**
Hall, Carrie, 8, 9, 11, 12, 21, 23, 26, 29, 34, **99**
Hallford, Mrs. Andy, **99**
Harbison, Mrs. W. L., 12
Harriman, Betty Harned, 11
Harriman, Elizabeth, **19**
Hatfield, America, 16
Hawaiian quilts and quilters, 17-18, 35, **62**, 114
Haynes, Sarah A., 31
Headlee, Hannah Haynes, 14, 25, 34, **55, 80, 125, 126**
*Hearth & Home*, 20, 31, **77**
"Hexagon Baskets," **82**
"Hexagonal Mosaic," **108**
"Hexagonal Stars," **94**
*Historic Quilts*, 12, 32, **111**
"Historic U.S.A.," **102**
Hobgood, Lois, 24
"Hollyhocks and Bluebirds," **44**
Holmes, Carlie Sexton, 11, 20
  and *Better Homes & Gardens*, 20
Home Art Studios, **69, 77**
Home Arts (syndicate), 21
*Home Arts Needlecraft*, **6**
"The Homestead," **113**
"Honeycomb," 29
"Honeymoon Cottage," **85**
Hoover, Herbert, **iv, v**
"Horn of Plenty, **95**
*House Beautiful, The*, 7, 25
*House in Good Taste, The*, 7
"House-on-the-Hill," **83**
Houston Quilt Festival, 1

Ickis, Marguerite, 12
"Indiana Wreath," **43**
Innes department store, 20
"Iris," **53**
"Iris Garland," **55**
"Irish Chain," 12, **107**

Jameson, Mrs., **100**
"Japanese Lanterns," **94**
JBK Company, The, **135**
J. C. Penney, 34

*Kansas City Star*, 1, 10, 13, 16, **64, 77, 93, 100**
"Kansas Pattern," **61**
Katzenberg, Dena, 10
Keefer, G. B., 23
Kendig, Harry D., 32

King, Elizabeth, 13-14
Kirk, E. Buchner, **131**
"Kittens," **65**
Kretsinger, Rose G., **ii**, 8, 9, 11, 12, 13, 14, 18, 20, 25, 36, **43, 80, 99**

"Labyrinth," **110**
*Ladies Art Catalog*, **76, 106**
Ladies Art Company, 10, 12, 20, 21, 25, 31
"The Ladies' Dream," 12
*Ladies' Home Journal, The*, 1, 10, 11, 16, 20, 34, **79**
"Lady with Butterfly," **135**
"Lady's Boot," **63**
LaGanke, Florence, **77, 127**, and see Nancy Page
Landon, Alfred M., 16, **101**
"Landon's Sunflower," 16
Langley, Mable, 24
Lap quilting, 11
Lathouse, Mrs. W.B., 12, **104, 105**
Laura Wheeler (syndicated column), **45, 51, 65, 67, 83**
"Leaves," **123**
Lee Wards, 23, **54**
Leman, Bonnie, 14, 23
Leman, Mary, 14
Leonhard, Emma Mae, **90**
Lichten, Frances, 5
*Life*, 5, 16
"Little Birds," 13
Living History Farms, 13
Lockport Batting, 20, 21
"Log Cabin" quilts, 10, **84, 97**
"Log Cabin-Courthouse Steps," **4**
"Log Cabin/Roman Stripe/Streak o' Lightning," **94**
Long, Jane, 29
"Louisville Male High School," 33

*McCall's*, 18, **19**, 34
McCoy, Rhoda, 16
McElwain, Mary A., 24, **129**
McKim, Ruby Short, 11, 14, 21, 34, **85**
McKim Studios, 14, 21, **59, 77**
Macy's, 1, 23, **54**
"Map of New York," **123**
"The Matterhorn," **117**
Meckstroth, Bertha, 24, 36
"A Meeting of the Sunbonnet Children," **30**
"Menagerie," **130**
"Mennonite Picnic," **117**
Mennonites, **117**
"Michigan Flower Pot," 13
Mickey Mouse and Minnie Mouse," **137**
"Miniaturized Postage Stamp," **109**
*Modern Priscilla*, 21, 34
Montgomery Ward, 20
"Morning Glory," **45**
"Mosaic" quilts, **108, 111**
"Mosaic Roses," **46**
"Motoring Lady," **135**
"Mountain Dreams," **115**
Mountain Mist, 1, **4**, 14, 16, 21, 23, **46, 47**
Museum of American Folk Art, 23, 25

Nancy Cabot (syndicate), 5, 14, 16, 21, 31, **50, 96**
Nancy Page (syndicate), 16, 21, **77, 85, 126, 129**
National Gallery of Art, 5
National Quilting Bee Contest, 23
"Navy Wives Quilt," 16, 34
*Needlecraft, the Magazine of Home Arts*, **4**
*Needlecraft Magazine*, **4**, 16
Needlecraft Supply Company, The, 24
"Nervous ladies," 9, 12, 35
*New York Daily News*, 45
New York World's Fair (1939-1940), 5, 24, 36
*Newsweek*, 5
"Ninety and Nine" quilts, 29, 33, **119**
Normann, Charles, **102**
Normann, Fanny, **102**
"Nosegay," 45
NRA (National Recovery Act), 14
NRA ("National Recovery Act"), **100**
"Nursery Rhyme," **132**

"Ocean Waves," 35
Old Chelsea Station Needlecraft Service (syndicate), 21, **44, 59, 106**
*Old Patchwork Quilts*, 11-12, **63**
*Old Quilts*, 9, 12
Oliver, Charlene, **77**
"Orchid Wreath," 14
"Oriental Poppy," 14
"Oriental Sunflower," 59
Orr, Anne, 11, 20, 21, 24, 25, **46, 47**
  and *Good Housekeeping*, 20, 24, 46
"Our Pride," 13
Outline embroidery, 33

"Painted Flowers," **47**
"Paradise Garden," **ii**, 12-13
Paragon Needlecraft, **22**
Paragon Pattern Company, **15, 58**
Parrish, Maxfield, 10
"Parrots," **106**
Patchwork, 1, 10, 26
  loss of interest in, 7
Pattern catalogues, 12, 18
  marketing of, 18, 20
Pattern designs, 6, 14, 16, 18
Pattern exchange, 10
  in marketplace, 10
"Peace with the Indians," **118**
"The Peacock," **125**
Pearce, Mrs. J. B., 23
Pearl, Metta McRoberts, 13
*People's Popular Monthly*, **77**
Peto, Florence, 5, 11, 12, 32, **111**
Phelps, Nan, **2**
"Pickle Dish," **69**
"Pictograph," **114**
*Pictorial Review*, 23
"Pictorial Yo-yo," **134**
Pieced work, 10, 26, 28, **61, 81, 88, 120, 121**
Pillow kits, **135**
"Pine Trees," **67**
"Pinwheel Sunflower," **59**

148

"Pot of Flowers" quilts, 13, **58**
"The Potted Tulip," 13, 23
*Practical Needlework Patterns*, 20
Pratt, Charles, 29, 33, **119**
"Pride of Iowa," 13
"Prince's Feather/Sunburst," **6**
Printed embroidery, 34
"Prosperity Is Just Around the Corner," **v**, 13

Quilt blocks, 21, 23, 25
Quilt designers, professional, 10–11
*Quilt Fair Comes to You, The*, 24
Quilt historian, 11
Quilt kits, ix, 5, **15**, 18, 21, 23, **23**, 47, 54, **129, 131**
*Quilt Pattern Index, The*, 37
Quilt patterns, published, ix, 5
"Quilt Show," 13, **120**
*Quilter's Newsletter Magazine*, 14, 23
Quilters Hall of Fame, 12
Quilting
  and era of change, 1
  and government policy, 5
  interest in, 7, 8
  as leisure activity, 10
  loss of enthusiasm for, 7, 34–35
  reasons for, 8, 9
"The Quilting Bee," **121**
Quilting bees, 8, 9, **9**, 10, 16, 17, 25, **84**
Quilting competitions, 23–24
Quiltmakers, professional, 25, 26
Quilts
  as art, 10–11
  books about, 11–12
  care of, 38
  and collecting, 36–37
  and department stores, 1, **4**, 14
  and displaying, 37–38
  as folk art, 10
  inspiration for, iv, 13–14
  and "name games," 16–17
  and newspapers, 1, 18, 20, 34, **127, 129**
  and patriotic motifs, 14
  and periodicals, 1, 18, 20, 34
  prices of, 5–6
  and talent of quiltmakers, 5
  and women's consciousness, **x**
*Quilts: Their Story and How to Make Them*, 11, 48, 49

"Rainbow Double Wedding Ring," **69**
Rainbow Quilt Company, 21
Red Cross, 16, **16**
Red Cross quilt, **98**
Reichard, Mrs. Emma, 33
Riley, Mrs. B. W., 109

Rising, Loretta Leitner, *see* Nancy Cabot
Roberds, Mrs. Pearl Willard, **91**
Robertson, Elizabeth Wells, 12
Rock River Cotton Company, 18, 21
"Roman Stripes–Log Cabin," **3**
*Romance of the Patchwork Quilt in America, The*, 8, 11, 12, 20, 99
Roosevelt, Eleanor, 1, 24, **24**, 103
Roosevelt, Franklin Delano, 12, 14, 16, **67**, **99, 101, 104, 105**
"The Roosevelt Rose," 16
"The Rose of the Field," 16
"Roses," **56**
Rowley, Louise, 12
Roy, Suzanne, 5
*Rural New Yorker*, 77

Sailing-ship motif, **135**, 136, **136**
St. Louis *Post-Dispatch*, 29
"Sampler," **122**
Savery children, **128**
"Sawtooth," **106**
"Schoolhouse" quilts, **84, 85**
"Scotties," **66**
"Sea Wings to Glory," 16
Sears, Roebuck, 1, **3**, 12, 18, 23, 24, **24**, 34, 36, **85**
Seton, Ernest Thompson, 10
"Shadow Boxes," **97**
Shaw, Fannie B., iv, **v**, 13
Shogren, Linda, 37
Small, Albert, 29, 32, **111**
Smith, Callie Jeffress Fanning, **103**
Smith, Jessie Willcox, 10
"Snail's Trail," **110**
Snyder, Grace McCance, 9, 36, **111, 112**
Snyder, Ruth, 20, 32
Soden, Mrs. S. J., **61**
"Spanish work," *see* "Blackwork"
"Spiderweb," **96**
"Spring Tulips," **44**
*Standard Book of Quiltmaking and Collecting, The*, 12
"Star of Bethlehem" quilts, **6, 77**
"Star of France," **74**
"Star Hexagons," **76**
"Stars and Stripes" quilts, **99, 104**
"Starburst" quilts, **75, 78**
State motifs, 31–32
Stearns & Foster, **4**, 21, 23, 37, **44, 46, 47, 48, 53, 54, 76, 95, 108**
Stenge, Bertha, 5, 13, 16, 18, 24–25, **120, 121**
Stone, Clara, 12, 20
  and *Hearth & Home*, 20
Stuffed work, **ii**, **x**, **43**, **99**, and *see trapunto*
"Summer Time 1933," **85**
*Sunbonnet Babies Primer, The*, 31

Sunbonnet Sue, 31, **88**
"Sunbonnet Sue" quilts, **89, 129**
"Sunflowers," **93**
"Swan and Deer," **130**
"Sweet Peas," **54**
Syndicated pattern companies, 21
Synthetic battings, 17

"Tea Cozy/Toaster Cover," **137**
"Tennis Lady," **135**
Textile paintings, **113**
Thate, Pearl, 32
Throckmorton, Jeannette, Dr., 36, **50**
*Trapunto*, **x**, 10, and *see* Stuffed work
"Tree of Life," **49**
"Trees," **63**
"Trees and Garlands," **127**
"Trolley Cars," **65**
"Tulip Garden," **60**
"Tulips" quilts, **51, 61**
"Turtles," **67**

"Umbrella," **62**
Unruh, Minnie, 26
"Urn of Flowers," **57**

"Variable Star," 12
"Vase of Flowers," 24
"Victory," 5, 24
"Victory" quilts, 34
  and V symbol, 16
"Victory Is Our Goal," **105**

Walker, Lillian, 11, 25, 36
"War Bride's Quilt," 16
"Water Lilies," **53**
Webster, Marie D., 11, 20, 21, 25, 26, 29, 31, 34, **43, 45, 48, 49,** 79
  and *Ladies' Home Journal, The*, 20, 34
Webster, Mrs. Noah, **85**
White, Mrs. Cecil, **115**
Whitehill, Charlotte Jane, 12, 13, 24, 25, **61, 125**
Wilkins, Achsah Goodwin, **ii**
Wilkinson Art Quilts, 26
"Windblown Tulips," **48**
W. L. M. Clark Co., 16
*Woman's Day*, 5, 16, 18, 24, 25, 34, 36, **49, 62**
*Woman's World*, 23, 56
"Women of All Nations," **92**
*Women's Home Companion*, **131**
"World of Tomorrow," **91**
World War II, 16, 25
WPA (Works Progress Administration), 5
WPA Index of American Design, 5, 11

# ABOUT THE AUTHORS

THOS. K. WOODARD and BLANCHE GREENSTEIN are co-owners of Thos. K. Woodard: American Antiques & Quilts, one of the best-known galleries in New York City specializing in nineteenth- and early twentieth-century quilts, folk art, and country furniture.

As coauthors of *Crib Quilts and Other Small Wonders* (1981) and *The Poster Book of Quilts* (1984), Mr. Woodard and Ms. Greenstein have addressed audiences at numerous museums, quilt festivals, and educational institutions. They served as guest curators for the Museum of American Folk Art's 1979 exhibition of Hawaiian quilts in New York City. Mr. Woodard writes on quilts as a guest columnist for *Country Living* magazine.

Mr. Woodard was raised in Des Moines, Iowa, and after graduating from the University of Kansas, came to New York where he served as box-office treasurer for the New York Shakespeare Festival.

Ms. Greenstein was born and raised in New York, and she is a graduate of New York University. A former stylist for photographers and television producers, Ms. Greenstein's interest in antique textiles began as a hobby, the genesis of what is now a leading source for quilt collectors in the United States, Canada, South America, Europe, Australia, and the Far East.